Uncle John's
BATHROOM READER®
CHRISTMAS
COLLECTION

Uncle John's BATHROOM READER® CHRISTMAS COLLECTION

Portable Press

San Diego, California

Uncle John's Bathroom Reader
Christmas Collection

For information, visit us at www.bathroomreader.com, or write to:
Uncle John's Bathroom Reader,
Portable Press, 5880 Oberlin Drive, San Diego, CA 92121,
e-mail: unclejohn@advmkt.com

Library of Congress Cataloging-in-Publication Data
Uncle John's bathroom reader Christmas collection.
p. cm.
ISBN 13: 978-1-59223-484-4
ISBN 10: 1-59223-484-4
1. Christmas. 2. Christmas--Humor. I. Title: Bathroom reader
Christmas collection. II. Title: Christmas collection.

GT4985.U54 2005
394.2663--dc22

2005053940

Printed in Canada
05 06 07 08 09   10 9 8 7 6 5 4 3 2

Project Team

Allen Orso, Publisher

JoAnn Padgett, Director, Editorial and Production

Amy Briggs, Project Editor

Jennifer Browning, Project Editor and Production Manager

Michael Brunsfeld, Cover Designer

Robin Kilrain, Copy Editor

Jennifer Connolly, Proofreader

Thank You!

We sincerely thank the following additional people whose
advice and assistance made this book possible.

Cynthia Francisco

Gordon Javna

Ellen O'Brien

Julia Papps

Sydney Stanley

Olivia Tabert

Jennifer Thornton

Connie Vazquez

Thank You Contributors!

We sincerely thank the following people who
contributed selections to this work.

Amy Briggs
Jennifer Browning
Myles Callum
Jenness Crawford
Kathleen Duey
Dan Erdman
Vickey Kalambakal
Robin Kilrain
Andy Levy-Ajzenkof
Art Montague
John Scalzi
Susan Steiner
Bobbye Terry
Stephanie Villanova
Julia Wittner

Contents

Finding Christmas

Here Comes Santa Claus

Ho! Ho! Ho!

Holiday History

Merry Miscellany

Seasonal Sounds

Signs of the Season

Tree Trimmings

Answer Pages 176

Introduction

Here at the Bathroom Reader, the Christmas season is a favorite time of year. So it's no surprise that we decided to create this book filled with so many of the beloved traditions of the season.

We couldn't pass up the story of the real-life Scrooge who found a way to preserve the holiday season back when most people had lost interest. We also knew this book wouldn't be complete without little Virginia's timeless 1897 Letter to the Editor—as well as the editor's eloquent reply that puts every Santa scoffer in his or her place.

You'll also find:

- A list of biggest tree trimmings that will make you rethink the phrase "keeping up with the Joneses."
- The History of Santa, where you'll learn the origin of Saint Nick and how his home went from Turkey to the North Pole.
- Some corny holiday jokes (we call them Yuletide Yuks) that'll make you groan, then chuckle, then maybe even want to share them with family and friends.

We've enjoyed every festive moment creating *Uncle John's Christmas Collection*. The biggest reason—it's given us a chance to reflect on our favorite things about this time of year.

Julia, our Ashland, Oregon, office manager loves that Christmas day is always so still; the buzz of life seems to drop several decibels. Amy, our developmental editor in San Diego, looks forward to watching the Christmas specials on TV. Jennifer, our production editor in San Diego, loves the music—carols on the radio, concerts by the orchestra, and the old classics still treasured on vinyl. JoAnn, the majordomo at the San Diego office, ever prolix but always eloquent, defined Christmas as:

- A time to deck the halls.
- A time to gather with family and friends.
- A time to enjoy the excitement on the faces of children.
- A time to believe.

It's hard to top that! We hope that, whether you are the giver or receiver of *Uncle John's Christmas Collection*, this little book will add some joy to your holiday season, as it has ours.

Merry Christmas!
Uncle Al

How Scrooge Saved Christmas

Christmas was being scrooged out of existence—until a ghost story came along to save it.

Everyone knows about Ebenezer Scrooge. He's that cold-hearted miser who won't let his employee, Bob Cratchit, celebrate Christmas. Fortunately, on Christmas Eve, the ghost of his partner, Jacob Marley, and the ghosts of Christmas Past, Present, and Yet to Come give Scrooge such a fright that he reforms and changes his money-grubbing ways. Okay, you know the story. But did you know that the tale of Scrooge not only changed the celebration of Christmas, it probably saved it from extinction?

On December 19, 1843, a slim, gilt-edged book, *A Christmas Carol,* by Charles Dickens, appeared in London bookshops. In that same year, no one wished each other a Merry Christmas. They'd probably never even heard the phrase. And Christmas itself had long since waned. Oliver Cromwell and his Puritans considered it a pagan holiday and in the 1640s began to pass various acts to restrict the celebration of Christmas. Even after the monarchy was restored in 1660 and many of the laws repealed, Christmas had been delivered a severe setback.

By winter 1843, the Industrial Revolution was hammering the final nails in the Christmas coffin. Folks had migrated to cities. The old country Christmas that had been celebrated for 12 festive days was already gone. Most urban employers, like old Scrooge, weren't about to give workers even one day off just to have a party with their families. The dying traditions of Christmas, it seemed, would soon be a quaint part of England's history—if they were remembered at all.

Charles "Scrooge" Dickens

When Dickens wrote *A Christmas Carol,* he made a plea for the renewal of the customs his own father had known— spiced wine punch, roast goose, and the warmth of Yule logs on a snowy Christmas night. But like Scrooge, what he hoped for was profit from his holiday tale. Dickens's parents had never been as warm and loving as the Cratchits. When Charles was 12, his careless father went to debtors' prison, and Dickens labored in a rat-infested boot-blacking factory. The dark memory made the author a reformer of workhouses and child labor laws. It helped him value family celebrations like the one he created in *A Christmas Carol.* It also made him desperate to be as rich as Scrooge.

In his push to make *A Christmas Carol* a best seller,

Dickens gave readings of his little book, sometimes for charity, often for a fee. Dickens was a wonderful storyteller and his readings did as much for Christmas as they did for his bank balance. "I feel," one factory owner said, "that after listening to Mr. Dickens's reading of *A Christmas Carol* tonight, I should break the custom we have hitherto observed of opening the works on Christmas Day."

Merry Christmas

As *A Christmas Carol* became beloved throughout the English-speaking world, Dickens's idea of how to celebrate Christmas caught on. People couldn't spend 12 days at it, but, like Bob Crachit, they could wish each other Merry Christmas. They could spend Christmas Eve and Christmas Day with their families. They could strive for good times and goodwill.

In 1870, so the story goes, a Cockney girl heard that Dickens was dead. She gasped, "Dickens dead? Then will Father Christmas die too?" The Ghost of Christmas Yet to Come would have been happy to tell her that Father Christmas would remain alive and well thanks to Charles Dickens.

The History of Santa, Part 1

We delved into The Best of Uncle John's *to learn all about Santa's history. Here's how an almost completely unknown bishop became the most recognized holiday character in Western civilization.*

In the 4th century A.D. a man named Nicholas became the bishop of a village called Myra in what is now Turkey. Little is known about him, but it's a pretty safe guess that he was a kind and generous man; legends attributed to him describe many kind acts toward children.

Bishop Nicholas of Myra was canonized and went on to become the most popular saint in all of Christianity. He is the patron saint of children, and more churches are named after him than any of the apostles. To honor him, Europeans began giving gifts to their children on the eve of the feast of Saint Nicholas, which falls on December 6.

Saint Nick Comes to America

During the Protestant Reformation, Saint Nicholas was replaced in many countries. In England he was known as Father Christmas, and in France he was called Père Noël. But Saint Nicholas remained popular in the Netherlands. On

Saint Nicholas's Eve, children would leave their wooden shoes filled with straw for the donkey on which he rode, and by morning the straw was replaced with presents. When the Dutch settled New Amsterdam in the fledgling New World, they brought their traditions with them.

In 1664, the flourishing colony of New Amsterdam was taken over by the British, who renamed it New York after the Duke of York. For the next 200 years or so, the Dutch citizens of the colony worked to preserve their culture and traditions. One of the most active groups was an association of Dutch intellectuals called the Knickerbockers.

Writer Washington Irving was a member of the group, and in 1809 he published a satirical book on Dutch traditions. It contained references to Sinter Klaas (an adaptation of Saint Nicholas), including a tale of how he flew across the sky in a wagon and dropped presents down chimneys for good little girls and boys—not just on Christmas, but on any day he felt like it. The English settlers loved the stories and enthusiastically adopted the Dutch celebrations of Saint Nicholas Day, but they gradually merged them with their own Christmas traditions. It's not hard to see how

Sinter Klaas became Santa Claus in the mouths of the English-speaking New Yorkers.

Santa Claus

When Clement Moore, a friend of Washington Irving, sat down to write his children a Christmas poem in 1822, he was heavily influenced by Irving's vision of Sinter Klaas and his flying wagon and gift giving. But Moore made a few alterations. The children now hung stockings, and the wagon became a "miniature sleigh" pulled by "eight tiny reindeer." A common sleigh pulled by reindeer gave Saint Nick an exotic link to a faraway land in the North—a mysterious land of cold and snow. Moore described a dwarfish "jolly old elf," dressed in furs, who goes down chimneys to give children gifts. He even gave the reindeer names: Dasher, Dancer, Prancer, Vixen, Comet, Cupid, Donder, and Blitzen. Other Christmas stories had portrayed Saint Nicholas on a white horse, or with one or two reindeers—one version even had him in a cart pulled by a goat—but Moore's account was so vivid and compelling that it became the standard.

Moore never intended for anyone other than his children to hear his poem "A Visit From Saint Nicholas." In fact, for more than 20 years he refused to admit he was the author (apparently he was afraid it would damage his standing in the academic community in which he was a professor of Oriental and Greek literature). But his wife liked the story so much that she sent copies to her friends, and somehow the poem was printed anonymously in the Troy, New York, *Sentinel* on December 23, 1823. It eventually became known as "The Night Before Christmas." The poem was so popular that within a decade it had become a central part of the Santa legend . . . as well as the best-known poem in American lore.

Turn to page 145 for more of the story.

The Making of "The Gift of the Magi"

O. Henry's "The Gift of the Magi" is among the best-known Christmas stories: Two desperately poor sweethearts buy each other Christmas gifts—he, combs for her hair; she, a chain for his watch—only to find that in order to buy those gifts, he sold his watch, and she sold her hair. As touching as the story is, however, it almost didn't exist at all.

Born in 1862, William Sydney Porter (pen name O. Henry) was a clever young writer who worked as a bank teller. Porter ran into trouble on the job and was convicted of embezzlement in 1897. Today there is some question about his actual guilt, but there was no question then, and he served time in prison. While there he began to write adventure tales to support his young daughter and began to use the name O. Henry. His first story, "Whistling Dick's Christmas Stocking," was written in 1899 to earn money to buy his daughter a Christmas present (a set of Uncle Remus stories). He served part of his five-year sentence and was released in 1901.

O. Henry arrived in New York in 1902, found a job

writing a story a week for the *New York World,* and did immensely well for himself—despite a reputation for procrastinating and missing deadlines.

You Supply the Picture, I'll Supply the Story

"The Gift of the Magi" was supposed to be the Christmas story for the *New York World*'s December 1905 issue, but O. Henry, true to his reputation, was late. The editor sent the story's illustrator to find O. Henry and see if any material was ready.

When the illustrator found O. Henry, he did not have even a draft or a plan. But the persistent illustrator begged for an image to draw so he could meet his deadlines. O. Henry agreed, and he set the scene: A poor, young man and woman, sitting in a small room and talking about Christmas. The man holds a watch fob in his hand. The woman has long, beautiful hair. And then Henry told the artist: "That's all I can think of now, but the story is coming."

The artist left, and Lindsey Denison, an editor with the *World*, arrived to babysit O. Henry and to make sure the story was written. The story was so late that as O. Henry finished pages, Denison had them set in type without any editing. The story was finished in less than three hours.

"Gift" became an instant American classic and has been called the "greatest of all Christmas stories which has . . .

come from the pen of an American writer." All from a desperate moment that could have been straight out of one of O. Henry's very own stories.

Afterword

Two restaurants in New York City claim to be the site where O. Henry wrote "The Gift of the Magi." Located at 55 Irving Place, Sal Anthony's Restaurant occupies the site of Henry's old apartment and has a plaque on the wall stating that he wrote the story there. The management at Pete's Tavern disagrees. Just up the block at 66 Irving Place, Pete's (called Healy's Cafe in O. Henry's day) says that "Gift" was conceived in the second booth on the right, near the side door. A framed copy of part of the handwritten manuscript hangs over the spot. Since no one will be able to verify the exact spot of the writing, the two establishments have "agreed to disagree."

"The magi, as you know, were wise men
—wonderfully wise men who brought
gifts to the Babe in the manger.
They invented the art of giving
Christmas presents."

—O. Henry, author

A Neiman Marcus Christmas

Fancy a hot air balloon, a mummy, even a submarine for Christmas? Neiman Marcus has just what you're looking for.

The Media Comes Calling

When Stanley Marcus became president and CEO of the Texas-based Neiman Marcus in 1950, he was under pressure to expand the thriving family business into other cities. Newsman Walter Cronkite inadvertently gave him an idea. The television anchor would routinely call the week before Christmas wondering what unique items the rich oil folks were buying. Sensing that Cronkite didn't want a plain answer, Marcus would exaggerate a little and tell Cronkite about a man who bought over-the-top, ultraextravagant gifts, like mink coats for all of his daughters.

It didn't take long for inspiration to follow. The store had been publishing its *Neiman Marcus Christmas Book* since 1939, a 16-page special catalog that was sent only to select customers and contained a treasure trove of gifts: fur coats, perfumes, toys, you name it. Marcus could use the catalog to sell these outlandish items, and the store would rake in endless media attention. Whether anyone bought them or not, the publicity would be priceless. The idea quickly developed into one of the store's most popular offerings . . . His and Hers gifts on a very grand scale.

What's on Your Wish List?

No idea was too outrageous: His and Hers bathtubs, airplanes, or gold-encrusted wigs. During a recession, Marcus thought up matching gifts for pessimists and optimists. The negative-minded could buy a made-to-order ark à la Noah, and the optimists could get oak seedlings. The rumor is that he sold 1,500 oaks and nary an ark.

Much to the credit of Mr. Marcus's business acumen and marketing savvy, the family retail business continued to thrive. The store expanded to include locations nationwide, and the His and Hers exclusives are as popular as ever. Here's a partial list of the zaniest gift ideas to date—and the retail price of each.

Year	Gift	Cost
1963	Mini-submarines, each	$18,700
1964	Hot air balloons, each	$6,850
1967	Camels, pair	$4,125
1971	Mummy cases, pair*	$6,000
1977	Windmills, each	$16,000
1979	Dirigibles, each	$50,000

1980	Baby ostriches, each	$1,500
1981	Robots, each	$15,000
1985	Diamonds, pair	$2,000,000
1991	LTV Hummer	$50,000
1997	Windjet	$32,600
2000	Rokkaku kites, pair	$2,000
2002	Personalized action figures	$7,500

In May 2005 Neiman Marcus Group, Inc. announced its plans to sell the company, which begs the question: What will become of the popular *Neiman Marcus Christmas Book* and the His and Hers gifts? President and CEO Burt Tansky reassures us that "it will be business an usual."

*For more on the mummy cases, see page 85.

Where does Kris Kringle fit in to the Santa mix? It's actually just a synonym, although the name has evolved over the years. Kris Kringle is an Americanized version of the German Christkindl, meaning "Christ child." Christkindl replaced Saint Nicholas as the primary gift bringer for parts of Germany, Austria, and Switzerland. Over time, the name has seen various iterations: Krischkindel, Kriss Kindle, Kriss Kinkle. By the time the classic movie *Miracle on 34th Street* named its protagonist Kris Kringle, the name had long been synonymous with Santa Claus.

Annual Animated Offerings:
A Triple-Threat Quiz

A little quiz to see how closely you watch your Christmas specials every year.

It's hard to believe, but the televised Christmas specials created by Arthur Rankin Jr. and Jules Bass have been holiday traditions for over 40 years. Rankin and Bass have used their distinctive stop-motion animation to tell the stories of Rudolph, Santa, Nestor, the baby New Year, and Jack Frost. Along with the low-tech animation, another hallmark of each special is a celebrity narrator to tell the tale. See if you can match up the famous voice, the show's title, and the character's name in this triple-threat quiz.

Match the Stars ... With Their Characters ...

1. Burl Ives
2. Fred Astaire
3. Buddy Hackett
4. Roger Miller
5. Red Skelton

I.   Father Time, keeper of time
II. Sam, a talking snowman
III. S. D. Kluger, a mailman
IV. Pardon-Me-Pete, the groundhog
V.   Speiltoe, Santa's donkey

And the Shows

A. *Santa Claus Is Comin' to Town*

The story behind how Santa Claus began delivering toys on Christmas Eve.

B. *Jack Frost*

Winter spirit Jack Frost becomes human for one day and falls in love with a mortal girl.

C. *Rudolph the Red-Nosed Reindeer*

The story of a misfit reindeer whose nonconformity saves Christmas.

D. *Nestor the Long-Eared Christmas Donkey*

The story of a misfit donkey who helps Mary and Joseph travel to Bethlehem.

E. *Rudolph's Shiny New Year*

The story of a misfit reindeer who must find and save Happy, the baby New Year.

Turn to page 176 for the answers.

"There's nothing sadder in this world than to awake Christmas morning and not be a child."

—*Erma Bombeck, columnist*

Yuletide Yuks

Yeah, we know they're dumb. But we're pretty sure they'll make you chuckle.

What do you call people who are afraid of Santa Claus?
Claustrophobic.

Why is getting Christmas presents for your kids just like a day at the office?
You do all the work, and the fat guy in the suit gets all the credit.

What happens if you eat the Christmas decorations?
You get tinselitus.

What do monkeys sing at Christmas?
"Jungle bells, jungle bells . . ."

What happens to you at Christmas?
Yule be happy!

How did the chickens dance at the Christmas party?
Chick to chick.

Foods of Fortune

Here's a handful of Christmas culinary traditions from around the globe and through the ages.

- Swiss grandmothers once peeled off 12 layers of an onion—one for each month—and filled them with salt on Christmas Eve. The next day, they knew the weather for the coming year: the layers with damp salt indicated rainy months.

- Find a coin in your piece of Christmas cake? You might want to invest it in lottery tickets; it's a sure sign you're going to get rich in the coming year. At least, that's the tradition in Serbia.

- In Sweden, Christmas dinner is topped off by hot rice pudding, with one almond hidden inside. The person who gets the almond will marry within the year.

- Norwegians take the custom a step further: Once the almond is found, everyone leaves a little pudding on their plate for the dead to eat, since they visit on Christmas night. Norwegians also used to put a little barley in their shoe and stick it under the bed for the ethereal Christmas goat. If he didn't get his barley, there'd be bad luck for a year.

- Croatian Kolach is a ring-shaped coffee cake with three candles: one to be lit on Christmas Eve, one on Christmas Day, and the last on New Year's Day. The cake is divvied up on January 6, and everyone's good luck for the next year depends on devouring their stale, hard piece of cake.

- Other traditions of Merry Old England: eating apples at midnight on Christmas Eve to bring good health; leaving a loaf of bread on the table after dinner on December 24 so that there would always be bread in the house next year; and "wassailing the trees"—by sprinkling them with cider from the wassail bowl—to nurture the next crop of apples.

"Christmas is the season for kindling
the fire of hospitality in the hall,
the genial flame of charity in the heart."

—*Washington Irving, writer*

10 Things You Didn't Know About *A Charlie Brown Christmas*

A Charlie Brown Christmas has taken viewers down a familiar path every year since 1965: Charlie Brown directs a Christmas play and hunts for the perfect tree, Linus expounds on the true meaning of Christmas, and Snoopy and the rest of the gang dance to the music of the Vince Guaraldi Trio. But these 10 unfamiliar bits of information are worth knowing, too.

1. Thank Coca-Cola for the special.

The special got underway after a Coca-Cola ad representative rang up producer Lee Mendelson in 1965. Mendelson had produced a 1963 documentary on *Peanuts* cartoonist Charles Schulz that featured short animated bits of the popular comic strip's characters; the Coca-Cola guy wanted to know if Mendelson had thought of making a Christmas special (which Coca-Cola would sponsor). "Of course I have," Mendelson lied. Then he and Schulz banged out the story idea the very next day.

2. The unedited version is seldom aired.

Early versions of the special featured prominent advertisements for Coca-Cola, including a scene in which Snoopy hurls Linus from the ice rink and into a Coca-Cola billboard. The billboard came out when other sponsors objected. (Later the FCC decided such advertising inside kid's programming was a no-no.) Other scenes (like a scene with the characters throwing snowballs at a can) were trimmed to make way for commercials and only recently restored to the broadcast and video versions.

3. There was supposed to be a laugh track.

CBS executives were big fans of the laugh track, a standard feature of all funny shows in the 1960s. But Charles Schulz nixed the idea: He wanted people to laugh when they felt like laughing, not when they were told to.

4. The kids' voices actually come from kids.

Even today it's extremely rare for animated shows to actually use child actors. For one, adult actors are able to read their lines, and for another, if production takes several years, voice changes aren't a concern. Nevertheless, Schulz insisted on real kids' voices for the show (except for Snoopy who was voiced by animator Bill Melendez). The result is the unique *Peanuts* vocal delivery, in which characters sound as if they are being fed their lines out of earshot. That's because they were; some were so young that they couldn't read.

5. The network was nervous about the religious content.

CBS folks were concerned that Schulz's use of actual Bible quotes in the special would turn off viewers. Schulz justified their inclusion by saying, "If we don't do it, who will?" Thus Linus recites from the book of Luke during the show. One other bit of trivia—Linus, who was famously attached to his security blanket, lets go of it when he tells the story of Jesus' birth.

6. *Charlie Brown* was popular from the start.

Despite CBS's concerns about the laugh track, kids' voices, and religious sentiment, *A Charlie Brown Christmas* was a hit. When it first aired on December 9, 1965, it captured half the television audience and was the #2 show for the week—only perennial champ *Bonanza* did better in the ratings.

7. Critics and viewers loved the show.

In addition to great ratings, the show was also recognized with an Emmy Award for Outstanding Children's Program and a Peabody Award for programming excellence. After that, CBS made it a holiday tradition at the network (at least until ABC snatched the special from the network in 2000 to show it on its stations and affiliates).

8. The show made Vince Guaraldi a star.

Guaraldi had already been a well-known jazz pianist and composer (his song "Cast Your Fate to the Wind" won a Grammy in 1963), but the special welded the Guaraldi Trio's sound to the *Peanuts* characters—especially "Linus and Lucy," the music played while the *Peanuts* gang dances. Guaraldi released three albums of *Peanuts* music and scored all the subsequent specials until his death in 1976. He'd finished recording his work for *It's Arbor Day, Charlie Brown* the afternoon of the day he died.

9. Homages show up all over the place.

The Simpsons have regularly parodied the kids' dancing scene in their Halloween specials and in at least one "couch bit" at the show's opening (in which the family dog dances like Snoopy until the family comes in). Kids put on the *Peanuts* dance moves in Nickelodeon's animated show *Jimmy Neutron: Boy Genius* in the episode featuring "Jimmy Neutron's President Day Dance Party."

10. But wait! There's more!

A Charlie Brown Christmas isn't the only *Peanuts* Christmas special. There are three others: 1992's *It's Christmastime Again, Charlie Brown;* 2002's *Charlie Brown's Christmas Tales;* and 2003's *I Want a Dog for Christmas, Charlie Brown.* Each is cute in its own way, but it's *A Charlie Brown Christmas* that remains the tried-and-true favorite.

Tree-mendous Trivia

Hesitant to buy a live Christmas tree? Relax. They're grown on farms these days—and we're not even close to running out. Here are some tree facts to relieve your conscience . . . and a few others to keep you reading.

- An estimated 25 to 30 million live Christmas trees are sold every holiday season in the United States.
- Ninety-eight percent of Christmas trees are grown on tree farms.
- In the United States, more than 10 million new Christmas trees are planted every year.
- More than 1 million acres of land have been planted with Christmas trees. On average, over 2,000 trees are planted per acre. Each acre provides the daily oxygen requirements for 18 people.
- Once harvested, up to three seedlings are planted to replace one harvested tree.
- Christmas trees generally take six to eight years to fully mature.

Christmas Tree History

- Franklin Piece was the first U.S. president to have a decorated Christmas tree in the White House.

- The first commercial Christmas tree lot in the United States was set up in New York City in 1851.

- Queen Victoria's husband, Prince Albert of Germany, is credited with bringing the Christmas tree tradition to England.

- Grover Cleveland was the first president to use electric lights on the White House Christmas tree.

Assorted Christmas Tree Facts

- In the first week after being cut, a Christmas tree will consume as much as a quart of water every day.

- A Christmas tree with sparse branches is commonly referred to as a "Charlie Brown" tree.

- Greenland has to import all of its Christmas trees.

If you received all the presents mentioned in the song "The Twelve Days of Christmas," you'd have 364 gifts.

The Cake That Doesn't Die

In 2002, Americans spent $16 million on more than 5 million fruitcakes. We don't know who's eating all those cakes, but we did find out how come they last so long.

Two days before Christmas in 2003, host Jay Leno of the *Tonight Show* sampled a fruitcake made in November 1878. (That's a 125-year-old cake!) The good lady who baked it died the following year, but her family wasn't about to eat the last fruitcake she ever made. So they passed it down through the generations, treating it more like a family heirloom. Her descendant safeguard the dessert, doling out precious slices on rare occasions.

Stewed and Potent

One hundred and twenty-five years may be a record, but some fruitcakes do stay edible for up to 25 years (*edible* being a very elastic and relative term). How is that? Well, they're soaked in alcohol from beginning to end. All that booze not only makes for some pretty happy bakers, but it kills mold as well.

Consider: Some of the best cooks start out by soaking the fruit—dried or fresh—in dark rum or port wine for up to a week. Many recipes then call for a cup or two of whiskey, rum, or brandy to be added to the batter.

90-Proof Cakes

After the cakes are baked, the party keeps going. Some recipes call for sprinkling the cake lightly with brandy once a week for two weeks, or soaking a cloth with liquor and wrapping it around the cake. We like the trick of an English cook best. She put a teacup in the middle of the cake while it baked so that a deep hole was formed. Then every week she filled the hole with a few jiggers of rum and let it soak through the cake.

For the Teetotalers

Not all fruitcake recipes require liquor; many cookbooks call for fruit juice or milk instead. These cakes last for months or years because they are stored in tight tins that let very little air in. No mold grows. Gourmands agree: These deserve to wind up in Manitou Springs. Manitou Springs? We'll explain.

Enjoy It . . . As Far as You Can Throw It

Unloved fruitcakes have put the town of Manitou Springs, Colorado, on the map. Every year in late winter, over 100 participants gather for the Great Fruitcake Toss and compete for prizes as they destroy, mangle, splatter, and pulverize unwanted cakes. Events include the hand toss, spatula relay races, and launches by mechanical means, like catapults. In 2004, pneumatic guns were added, and air cannons propelled fruitcakes hundreds of feet into the air and into neighboring parking lots.

Before driving to Manitou Springs, you might want to check your vehicle's insurance coverage. Some fruitcakes we've tasted could put a pretty serious dent in the hood.

Fruitcake Musings

"The worst gift is a fruitcake.
There is only one fruitcake in the entire world,
and people keep sending it to each other."
—*Johnny Carson, comedian*

"You can take the rum out of a fruitcake,
but you still have a fruitcake."
—*Anonymous*

"The easiest way to make a fruitcake is to buy
a darkish cake, then pound some old, hard fruit
into it with a mallet. Be sure to wear safety glasses."
—*Dave Barry, columnist*

The Story of "Silent Night"

At one time or another, Haydn, Mozart, and Beethoven were each assumed to be the creators of the carol "Silent Night." After all, the melody is so beautiful in its simplicity it seems that only one of the great composers could be its mastermind. But we were all duped—for almost 200 years.

The story begins just before a Christmas Eve service in Oberndorf, Austria, in 1816. Josef Mohr, the assistant pastor, had written the poem "Stille Nacht! Heilege Nache" the previous year, and now he wanted it set to music for midnight Mass. Legend has it that mice had gnawed through the bellows of the organ. (Scholars have since discredited the story, suggesting instead that the organ simply was not working properly.) Whatever the reason, the organ was out of commission, and a solution had to be found.

Undaunted, Mohr asked the choir director and church organist, Franz Gruber, to set the poem to a guitar accompaniment instead. (A close variation of that melody is the one we know today.) The two sang each verse as a duet that night, and the choir joined in for the last two lines of each verse in four-part harmony; it was a modest, unassuming world premiere.

All Around the World

After the holiday, a traveling organ repairman came to
Oberndorf to fix the beleaguered organ. He obtained a copy
of the manuscript to take with him. It quickly became a popular Tyrolean folk song when two families of folk singers
added it to their repertoire—and slightly altered the melody.
From Austria, the little carol began its journey around
Europe and Russia. It was performed before royalty and com-
moners alike in great cathedrals and humble halls. "Silent
Night" was first performed in the United States in 1839, outside Trinity Church in New York City.

Where Credit Is Due

Over time and across nations, the true identities of the lyri-
cist and composer of the now famous "Silent Night" were
lost. This is not surprising, given the inconspicuous lives of
both Mohr and Gruber. Franz Gruber attempted to set the
record straight with music authorities in Berlin (he even
wrote several orchestral arrange-
ments of the melody over
the years), but the creative
genius for the piece was
invariably assumed to
be one of the great
composers. In the
mid-1990s, however,

the myth was officially dispelled when an original manuscript of the music was discovered and authenticated. Mohr
had written in the upper right-hand corner "Melodie von
Fr. Xav. Gruber."

Today, the little carol is performed each holiday season
more often than any other carol in the Christmas canon. It
has been translated into more than 300 languages.

During the Communist regime, Bulgarians were
required to give up all religious celebrations. So, eager to
keep their traditions and appease the new government at the
same time, they dropped the holy day on December 25 and
invented a very similar secular holiday on December 26.
Since the fall of the iron curtain, religious holidays were reinstated, but the Bulgarians have opted, thus far, to celebrate
Christmas on both days. Why not?

The people of Norway have donated a Norwegian
spruce to the people of London every year since 1947 as a
sign of gratitude for Britain's support during World War II.
The tree is the central part of the Trafalgar Square decorations and is taken down on the Twelfth Night of Christmas
(January 6).

You Better Watch Out

Halloween isn't the only holiday with things to be afraid of. It turns out that the Yuletide season has its fair share of characters to watch out for—especially if you've been naughty this year.

The Christmas Cat

Hailing from Iceland, this cat eats children who don't get new clothes for Christmas. Why? Because these are the children who didn't help out with spinning and knitting during the year, and the Christmas Cat knows that lazy children are the tastiest.

Julenissen

These gnomes of Scandinavian origin are pretty harmless, as long as they are bribed with a bowl of rice pudding on Christmas Eve. If the pudding isn't delivered, the Julenissen will cause lots of household mischief.

Knecht Ruprecht

This intimidating helper of Saint Nicholas comes from Germany and goes by many names. A tall, imposing figure, Ruprecht dresses in long, brown robes; sports a long, tangled, dark beard; has a sooty face; and carries a big stick to punish bad children.

Klaubauf

On Saint Nicholas Day (December 6), it's hard to miss Klaubauf, an Austrian Saint Nicholas helper. His shaggy coat, goat horns, long red tongue, and rattling chains make him easy to spot—but hard to avoid for a disagreeable child.

Krampus

A horned monster with a whip, Krampus travels around Central Europe with Saint Nicholas to scare badly behaved children into becoming good ones. On his back, he wears a wooden basket in which to throw misbehavers, but legend says that Saint Nicholas will intercede before Krampus can carry them off.

Oskorei

In Norway, best beware the Oskorei, mischievous spirits that can cause serious problems during Christmastime. Whether ruining the beer supply or attacking humans who walk alone at night, the Oskorei can be thwarted by painting crosses on barns.

Père Fouettard

In France, naughty children had better beware Père Fouettard (his name translates to Father Whip), who travels with Père Noël. This duo fall into a good cop–bad cop relationship; Père Noël rewards good children with presents, and Père Fouettard gives the bad ones spankings.

Schmutzli

Like his German counterpart Knecht Ruprecht, Schmutzli dresses in brown robes; has a long, brown beard and a dirty face; and carries a switch. But there's one big difference with this Swiss helper of Saint Nick. He doesn't just carry disagreeable children away—he eats them.

Have a Slangy Christmas

- In the American South, Christmas can mean whiskey—as in, "Pour a little Christmas in that eggnog, darlin'."

- CB radio–users don't like to get Christmas cards—that's a code name for speeding tickets.

- Loggers in the Pacific Northwest love Christmas: It means "payday."

- If an Aussie says, "You don't know Christmas from Bourke Street!"—you've just been called stupid.

The Magic Screen

A popular Christmas toy the day it was placed on the shelves, Etch A Sketch remains a classic today. We decided to share this toy story from Uncle John's Ahh-Inspiring Bathroom Reader.

In 1958 a 37-year-old Parisian garage mechanic named Arthur Granjean invented an amazing new toy. He called it L'Ecran Magique (Magic Screen). The Magic Screen was an unusual toy for its time—it didn't have a lot of little pieces that could get lost, and it didn't need batteries. Granjean felt sure his creation would interest someone at the International Toy Fair in Nuremberg, Germany. But everyone passed on it . . . until executives from a small American toy firm, the Ohio Art Company, took a second look. That did it.

Ohio Art bought the rights for $25,000 and renamed it Etch A Sketch. Then they advertised it on TV—just in time for the 1960 Christmas season—and sales took off. The response was so great that they kept the factory open until noon on Christmas Eve desperately trying to fill orders. They've never really slowed down.

Etch A Sketch Trivia

- **How many?** Some 8,000 Etch A Sketch toys are sold every day.

- **World's largest Etch A Sketch.** Steve Jacobs created the largest Etch A Sketch at the Black Rock Arts Festival in California in 1997. He placed 144 regulation-sized Etch A Sketches in a huge square and surrounded them with a huge red Etch A Sketch frame, including huge white knobs. It qualified for a Guinness World Record.

- **Expensive toy.** To celebrate the toy's 25th anniversary in 1985, Ohio Art came out with an executive model made of silver. The drawing knobs were set with sapphires and topazes. Price: $3,750.

- **Robot Etch A Sketch.** A Canadian computer programmer named Neil Fraser pulled the knobs off a standard Etch A Sketch and hooked it up to two motors that were attached to the port of his computer. The motors worked by remote control, enabling Fraser to draw pictures without ever touching the toy. Other robotic components tilted the Etch A Sketch upside down and shook it.

- **Extreme Etch A Sketch.** George Vlosich was 10 years old in 1989 when, on a long drive from Ohio to Washington, D.C., he brought along his Etch A Sketch. On the way home, he drew a sketch of the Capitol that was so good his parents photographed it. An artist was born. George soon began sketching portraits of his favorite sports heroes, then waited after games to get them to autograph his Etch A Sketch. The Etch A Sketch Kid started getting so much media attention that in 2000, Ohio Art sent someone to his home to see if he lived up to his reputation. They were so impressed by his talent that they've been supplying him with free Etch A Sketches ever since. It takes George between 40 and 60 hours to complete a single Etch A Sketch masterpiece. After it's done, he carefully unscrews the back and removes the excess aluminum powder to preserve the picture forever. His Etch A Sketch artwork sells for up to $5,000 each.

Though most Christmas trees end up as mulch or compost, in Bradley Beach, New Jersey, the trees are recycled for a more unique use. An estimated 19,000 trees have been used thus far to construct dunes along a mile-long stretch of oceanfront. With nor'easters depleting the beach's sand, the Christmas trees catch the blowing sand, eventually become buried, and turn into permanent dunes. To help keep the trees anchored, 50,000 plugs of dune grass have also been planted.

Boxing Day 101

In the United States, the day after Christmas is simply the day after Christmas. In the UK, however, it is Boxing Day: a holiday in its own right.

Tip Till You Flip

Boxing Day is December 26. Traditionally this is when all the haves distribute gifts and money to the have-nots who provide services throughout the year. Cabbies, street sweepers, waiters, lamplighters, milkmen, errand runners, newsboys—you name it. Think of it as a Victorian orgy of tipping—though it actually goes back much further than Victoria's reign. A 16th-century abbess, for instance, wrote about giving money to her kitchen clerk, servants, the gardener, and the "Baily of the Husbandry," whatever that was.

Not everyone was crazy about the Boxing Day tipping frenzy. Jonathan Smith—who wrote *Gulliver's Travels*—was quite put out when the Boxing Day tips to his coffeehouse attendants doubled. He had to pay, or else he'd look like a cheapskate in front of his friends. That was nearly 200 years ago—something to think about next time you drop some change at Starbucks.

Why Call It *Boxing Day*?

There are innumerable theories about where the name *Boxing Day* comes from, but no evidence to back up any of them. Here's a list of the most commonly encountered origin stories—feel free to insert *maybe* at the beginning of every sentence:

- Churches have locked boxes with slots in them to collect money for the poor. Called alms boxes, they may have been opened on December 26 and the contents distributed to the needy on that day.

- Church alms boxes may date back to imperial Rome. The Romans had a holiday called Paganalia to celebrate the crops sown in winter. The holiday came to England with the Roman conquerors. As part of the festivities, towns set up altars, and everyone piled coins for the poor on them.

- Apprentices carried earthenware boxes around to collect pay owed to their masters. They used the same type of box at Christmas to ask for tips for their good service.

- In 1703, one John Dunton speculated that the term *Boxing Day* came from the days when ships carried locked boxes holding offerings to the ship's patron saint. Before the ship sailed, everyone contributed a few pence, and no one could touch the box until the ship returned home safely.

The Weird Stuff

As with Christmas, some odd customs developed around the day. Horses were exercised and then bled on December 26, to keep them healthy throughout the year. Until the sport was banned in England in 2005, fox hunting meets took place on Boxing Day. These traditions may be connected to the fact that December 26 is also the feast day of Saint Stephen, who is the patron saint of horses—though no one knows why. (Stephen was the first Christian martyr back in the 1st century and had nothing whatsoever to do with horses.)

Boxing Day was traditionally a big night for theaters, since all the workers had some extra cash in their pockets. Pantomimes were introduced that night, and to this day mummers' performances occur all over England on Boxing Day weekend.

In some counties, a Saint Stephen's breakfast of beef and beer is put out for all takers. In Ireland, roving boys will carry around a dead wren, asking for money to bury it.

Why hasn't the rest of the world adopted this charming holiday? After all, pouring out money for gifts and tips on the day after Christmas, bleeding horses, watching mimes, and carrying dead birds around sounds pretty appealing. The rest of us just don't know what we're missing!

It's a Wonderful List

A wealth of little-known facts about a timeless Christmas classic.

The Film

- *It's a Wonderful Life* was released in 1946 by Frank Capra's newly formed Liberty Films. It was the studio's only production—and the only time Capra produced, financed, directed, and cowrote one of his films.

- The film was popular enough to be rereleased several times and performed on the radio with its original leads. But it didn't make as much money as a new Jimmy Stewart/Frank Capra film should have for a number of reasons: It opened late in December. Some of the movie's darker aspects, an attempted suicide and a child beating, turned moviegoers off. And the film wasn't as relevant as the war picture *The Best Years of Our Lives,* which won seven Oscars that year, including Best Picture.

The Script

- The movie is based on Philip Van Doren Stern's short story "The Greatest Gift." When the author's agent received a condensed version of it with his Christmas card, he pitched it to RKO Pictures, who bought it three months later. But the script was only partially developed and then shelved until Liberty Films bought it from RKO.

- Remember when Uncle Billy stumbles drunkenly out of George's house during Harry's homecoming party and it sounds like he's falling over some trash cans? Crew member Thomas Mitchell accidentally dropped some equipment backstage, but the actors stayed in character and filming continued—even when Mitchell shouted, "I'm all right, I'm all right." Capra left it all in the final cut and gave the clumsy stagehand an extra 10 dollars for "improving the sound."

- In the original script, the villainous Potter undergoes a change of heart. He turns up at the Baileys' doorstep with the missing money, but he's too ashamed to go in.

- The film originally ended as the Baileys and their friends sang "Ode to Joy," not "Auld Lang Syne," and recited the Lord's Prayer.

The Set

- It wasn't emotional turmoil that made Jimmy Stewart sweat so profusely during the dramatic bridge scene when George Bailey decides to commit suicide. It was 90 degrees the day that "snowy" scene was shot on the studio back lot.

- The Bedford Falls set was one of the longest ever built for an American film. Main Street was 300 yards long (three city blocks) and included 75 storefronts. The bank had a marble front, a rubber tile floor, and real cashiers' cages.

- The film didn't win any Oscars, but the effects department received a special award for creating a new type of film snow—soap and water mixed with the fire-fighting chemical Foamite pumped at high pressure through a wind machine. The new snow was silent and allowed for live sound recording, as opposed to the noisy cornflakes painted white that were used before.

The Cast

- RKO developed the part of George Bailey with Cary Grant in mind. When Capra bought the script from RKO, he wanted Jimmy Stewart for the lead.

- Uncle Billy's pet raven, Jimmy, appeared in all of Capra's pictures beginning with *You Can't Take It With You* in 1938. Capra cut a scene in which Jimmy attacks the dastardly Potter.

- Capra's early choice for Mary Bailey was Jean Arthur. RKO had wanted the role to go to Ginger Rogers. When Jean Arthur declined the role, Capra made the character more sweet and vulnerable and cast Donna Reed, whom he borrowed from MGM.

- Lionel Barrymore, who played Mr. Potter, was well known for his radio role as Scrooge throughout the 1930s. Another screen baddie, Vincent Price, was also considered for the role of Potter.

- Henry Travers, who played guardian angel Clarence, was considered for the roles of Peter Bailey, George's father; Mr. Gower, the druggist; and Uncle Billy. Interestingly, Travers played the Scrooge-like Horace P. Bogardus in *The Bells of St. Mary's*—the film listed on the marquee of the Bedford Falls movie theater.

- That freckle-faced fellow who opens up the pool in the gym during the Charleston dance scene is none other than 19-year-old Carl Switzer, aka Alfalfa from *Our Gang*.

Christmas Myth: The day after Thanksgiving (aka Black Friday) is America's top holiday shopping day of the year. **Fact:** Historically, the numbers simply don't bear this out. The biggest sales day is usually the last Saturday before Christmas. At best, Black Friday is only the fifth busiest day on average.

An Academy-award-winning Christmas performance as best supporting actor was turned in by Edmund Gwenn for his portrayal of Kris Kringle in *Miracle on 34th Street* (1947). Upon receiving his award he quipped, "Now I know there is a Santa Claus."

Yuletide by the British Book

In Great Britain, some old Christmas laws are still in effect. Here are some interesting ones—along with the years they were enacted.

1541 The Unlawful Games Act prohibits anyone from playing sports on Yuletide—except archery.

1551 The Holy Days and Fasting Days Act requires every citizen to attend church on Christmas Day—and to walk to and from. Anyone caught using a vehicle will have it confiscated and sold; proceeds will go to charity.

1625 It is illegal to gather a group of people together for any type of entertainment during the holiday.

1646 No Christmas dinner can have more than three courses, and absolutely no mince pie or Christmas pudding may be served.

1667 No working on Christmas Day. Period.

1831 Put away the guns; there's to be no hunting, either.

O Evergleam

Christmas decor in the 1960s took on a whole new look—in the form of aluminum trees.

Aluminum Christmas trees were not just a figment of Charles Schulz's imagination. Originally sold to department stores for use in holiday displays, in 1958 they caught the attention of the Aluminum Specialty Company in Manitowoc, Wisconsin, which recognized a progressive new look for an old-timey holiday. In 1959, the Evergleam hit the stores—and quickly hit the big time.

Silver Trees

The trees were popular for a number of reasons. The first and probably most obvious of these was convenience—the watchword of the new consumer age. The introduction of aluminum trees eliminated the hassle normally associated with Christmas trees—felling a tree, getting needles everywhere, hauling it to the curb in mid-January—and replaced it with a simple one-time visit to the department store. But the true secret of the aluminum tree's appeal was the sleek, modern sheen that it brought to the old-fashioned holiday. The 1960s marked the dawn of the space age, and perpetual progress was the order of the day. Most artifacts from this era—from chrome on car fenders to futuristic kitchen appliances—were shiny and metallic. So it was only natural for *der* Tannenbaum to take on the same appearance.

Many further refinements were introduced to add to the Aluminum Specialty tree's futuristic aura. In lieu of a decorative string of lights (since it's always a risky proposition to combine a chain of electric lights with several tiny metal strips), the company introduced a floor lamp that shined colored light onto the tree. With a rotating color wheel, consumers could switch between four different hues for their tree, which would reflect the color back in all of its metallic brilliance. A later innovation in a similar vein was a rotating tree stand, which slowly twirled the Evergleam on its base.

Back to the Future

Unfortunately, the tree's popularity was not to last. The post-war faith in endless progress through science and industry cracked in the late 1960s. The hippies and flower children of the new era preferred macramé to cool, sleek aluminum, paving the way for the earth tones of the 1970s, when space-age design seemed terminally square.

But these things go in cycles. As early 1960s "cool" has become fashionable once again, vintage aluminum trees have made a comeback. Two artists and Evergleam aficionados from Manitowoc, Wisconsin, John Shimon and Julie Lindemann, filled their studio with dozens of discarded, borrowed, or scavenged metal trees, creating an "aluminum forest" during the 1993 holiday season. This tribute to the town's manufacturing past drew an unexpected crowd, including many people offering to buy the trees (which weren't for sale).

In recent years collectors have shelled out big bucks for the original trees. A rare pink tree went for $1,200 on eBay in 2003. And new models are also being manufactured, much to the delight of modern-design junkies everywhere. The space age may be gone for the other 364 days of the year, but for one very special night, those who miss it—or missed out on it—can bask in the artificial glow of a tree that feels a little out of this world.

"Santa has the right idea. Visit people once a year."

—*Victor Borge, musician/comedian*

Christmas Music for the Naughty

Has someone been a bad little boy or girl this year? Don't give them a lump of coal: We've got a more appropriate punishment in mind—the gift of bad holiday music.

Hung for the Holidays

On one hand, it's hard not to be amused by William Hung, the earnestly rotten singer rejected from *American Idol.* His enthusiasm almost makes up for absolute singing incompetence and did make him one of the shows most surprisingly successful rejects; he has two albums to his credit (which is one more than Justin Guarini, by the way). But on the other hand, actually listening to Hung's covers of "Little Drummer Boy" and "Winter Wonderland" may have dried up a lot of goodwill toward him. In the words of one reviewer, "The suicide rate during the holiday season climbs high enough without Hung's help."

Christmas in the Stars

The worst thing about the *Star Wars Christmas* album is not C-3P0 (voiced by Anthony Daniels) discoursing on mathematical probability in "The Odds Against Christmas" or the song that has you pondering "What Can You Get a Wookie For Christmas (When He Already Owns a Comb)." (The answer: conditioner, and lots of it.) No, the worst thing about this album is that one of the singer's voices sounds eerily familiar. And then it hits you—that's Jon Bon Jovi singing "R2-D2, We Wish You a Merry Christmas." (It was Bon Jovi's first recording gig.)

A John Waters Christmas

When Waters, a devotee of all things camp, and the director of *Hairspray, Polyester,* and *Pink Flamingos* puts together a Christmas album, it's not going to be your average holiday outing. Tiny Tim trills his way through "Rudolph the Red-Nosed Reindeer," and Rudolph and the gang complain about Santa's weight in "Here Comes Fatty Claus." No matter how bad the music, Waters has only the best of intentions and wishes everyone a "merry, rotten, scary, sexy, biracial, ludicrous, happy little Christmas."

O Christmas Tree?

The phrase "Christmas tree" can mean just about anything. It all depends on where you are.

- If the captain of a ship or submarine told you to check the Christmas tree, you'd look at the nearest control panel, with all its red and green lights.

- On certain military planes, check the cluster rocket launchers under the wing.

- If you're in Congress, look for a bill with a bunch of unrelated riders decorating it . . . like an early Christmas present to lobbyists.

- Drag racers watch their side of a Christmas tree—with amber, green, and a final, red light—to count down to the start of the race.

- On an oil well, the Christmas tree is just below ground level, where valves cap the flow of oil.

- To computer hackers, a Christmas tree packet is a package of instructions that includes options for every conceivable protocol.

- Desperate students taking a multiple-choice test might Christmas-tree the answer sheet, by marking answers that will form the pattern of a Christmas tree.

- If someone yells, "Look at the Christmas tree!" at a bowling alley, high-fiving them would be inappropriate. A Christmas tree is a nasty split: the 7–10, with the 1, 2, or 3 pin left standing as well.

- You probably know that "all dressed up like a Christmas tree" means you're looking fancy, but how about this one: "All dressed up in Christmas tree order"? British soldiers used to say that in World War I. It meant the troops were in full-dress marching order. For some regiments, that meant kilts.

In a quest to find Great Britain's ultimate Santa, organizers at Guinness World Records sponsored the first-ever Santathon in December 2001. The event included a field of eight top contenders donned in full beards, red suits, and black boots. Competitive events included sack hauling, pie eating, chimney climbing, stocking filling, and ho-ho-hoing. First prize was awarded to David Broughton-Davis, 43, from Croydon, a professional department store Santa.

Mistletoe Demystified

If you pass under a door frame during the Christmas season you're sure to see a sprig of mistletoe over your head. And if you're not careful, someone is likely to smooch you.

According to botanists, mistletoe is a parasitic plant—it doesn't have true roots, it just attaches itself where it can grow, which is generally on oak and apple trees. Known scientifically as *Phoradendron flavescens* or *Viscum album,* mistletoe has oval, green, leathery leaves with either white or red berries. The name itself is derived from two Anglo-Saxon words that literally mean "twig dung," owing to the belief among early cultures that mistletoe seeds were spread from tree to tree in bird droppings—a theory since confirmed by modern scientists.

It's Norse, of Course

But how did a plant with such lowly origins turn into an instrument of Yuletide romance? According to Norse legend, mistletoe was closely associated with Frigga, the goddess of love and mother to Baldur, the god of the summer sun. Frigga was a protective mother who asked the elements of the earth as well as the animals and plants not to harm Baldur. But the mischievous Loki, the god of evil and a master of loopholes, knew Frigga had neglected to receive a pledge of loyalty from mistletoe, since it was a rootless plant that grew neither on nor under the earth. Equipped with this knowledge, Loki tricked Baldur's blind brother into shooting Baldur with an arrow tip tainted with the plant. Baldur was killed instantly, and the world plunged into darkness. Three days later, in mourning for her son, Frigga's tears were said to have changed the berries on a sprig of mistletoe from red to white, and Baldur was resurrected. Frigga was so grateful to have her son back that she kissed everyone who passed beneath the tree where the mistletoe grew.

We've Come a Long Way, Baby

Until the mid-1800s, the kissing custom seems to have been popular among the working class. Today, we all do it—we just need hanging greenery and someone to kiss. Proper mistletoe etiquette calls for the man to remove a berry from the cluster every time he kisses a woman under the greenery. When all the berries are gone, kissing under the mistletoe comes to an end for the season.

According to statistics, one in five people leave their Christmas shopping until the last week.

Santa Goes Bad . . .
In the Movies

*Tired of the malls? Sick of wrapping presents? Sometimes all that
Christmas spirit can get on your nerves. Luckily, there are plenty of
movies out there to solve that problem.*

Bad Santa (2003)

The name says it all. It's hard to beat Billy Bob Thornton's
turn as a drunken, abusive, department store Santa whose
surliness only barely masks his felonious intent (he and his
elf helper are casing the joint to rob it). After watching
Billy Bob, it might be hard to think of Santa as jolly ever
again.

The Nightmare Before Christmas (1993)

In this animated film, pumpkin king Jack Skellington who
rules Halloween Town has grown bored with tricks and
treats. One day he ventures into Christmas Town and,
delighted by what he sees, decides to run Christmas. He kid-
naps Santa Claus, dons the red suit, and begins dispensing
Christmas gifts created not by elves but by vampires, zom-
bies, and werewolves. Jack's Santa efforts fall flat because his

scary toys (fanged teddy bears, shrunken heads, and evil duckies) terrify rather than delight.

How the Grinch Stole Christmas! (1966)

Featuring one of the original (and best) bad Santas, this 1966 animated TV special brings to life Dr. Seuss's tale of a bad Santa who tries to stop Christmas from coming. Narrated by the creepy Boris Karloff (who also plays the Grinch), it tells the story of how the Grinch impersonates the real Santa to steal Christmas (he even takes the last can of Who Hash!). Best of all is the song "You're a Mean One, Mr. Grinch," memorably sung by Thurl Ravenscroft (who also voiced Tony the Tiger), which sums up all the no-good aspects of the Grinch: "The three best words that describe you are, and I quote, 'Stink, Stank, Stunk.'"

Silent Night, Deadly Night (1984)

If thieving Santas and Grinchy Clauses aren't bad enough for you, then slasher Santas might be in order. In this movie, an abused teenager dons the Santa suit to hack and chop his way through, well, just about everyone. Protested when it first came out by parents who objected to a murderous Santa, the movie's since become a hit on video, which explains the four straight-to-video sequels created between 1987 and 1992. Yes, you could have a slasher Santa marathon! But expect coal in your stocking if you do.

Hallelujah!

The Messiah is Handel's most famous work, the most popular oratorio in the world, and a fixture of the Christmas season. We thought we knew everything there is to know about it. But we were wrong. Here's what Uncle John found out.

Right Piece, Wrong Time

The Yule logs are burning, the holly is hung, and it's time to dig out those old *Messiah* scores, right? That's not what Handel had in mind when he wrote them. George Frideric Handel wrote the *Messiah* for Lent, and it debuted on April 13, 1742, the Tuesday before Easter, in a small theater in Dublin. Starting in 1745, the performance of the *Messiah* became an annual event in Dublin during Holy Week. Only when it crossed the Atlantic in the 19th century did performances of the *Messiah* become associated with the Christmas season. Most of these performances comprise only the first part, or Christmas section, with the "Hallelujah Chorus" tacked on for good measure. Even people who've sung the *Messiah* for years can't hum "Since by Man Came Death" from the third part.

Cast of Thousands

If you've been to any of the many professional productions of the *Messiah* you probably think the "Hallelujah Chorus" is meant to be sung by at least 100 singers, preferably as many as can fit on the stage. Actually, the original performance had only about 27 choristers, accompanied by a small string orchestra. These singers were members of the combined choirs of two cathedrals and were probably the only qualified singers Handel could find in Dublin.

The tradition of the enormous chorus started with the first Handel Centenary Commemoration concert in 1784 in London. For this event, 4,000 people crowded into Westminster Abbey to hear 513 performers play the *Messiah*. The organizers of the event were far more interested in promoting it as the largest choir ever assembled than in historical authenticity.

Will the Real *Messiah* Please Stand Up?

If you want to produce an authentic version of the *Messiah*, good luck. Handel himself constantly futzed with it, resetting lyrics, rewriting arias and recitatives for whichever soloists were available, and adding finishing touches here and there. There is no definitive musical text.

Slow and Steady Doesn't Always Win

Handel wrote the *Messiah* in just three weeks. This was not unusual for him—he dashed off most of his compositions just as quickly. Handel cut a few corners to churn out this piece, though. He adapted some Italian chamber duets he had been working on to serve as choruses in the *Messiah*. The original lyric, to the melody of "For Unto Us a Child Is Born" was "No, I don't trust you blind Cupid!" (in Italian, of course).

In the Beginning Were the Words

Charles Jennens, a literary scholar, assembled the libretto for the *Messiah* out of Old and New Testament scripture. He intended it to be his masterpiece. When Jennens got a chance to look at the finished *Messiah,* he was extremely disappointed with the music. He declared that "there are some passages far unworthy of Handel but much more unworthy of the *Messiah*." Jennens particularly abhorred the overture. Handel made some modifications after receiving an onslaught of letters from Jennens, but steadfastly refused to touch the overture. This led Jennens to melodramatically write to a friend, "I shall put no more Sacred Works into his hands, to be thus abus'd."

The Sacred vs. the Profane

Despite Handel's popularity in London, finding a venue for the *Messiah* was no easy task. Handel always considered opera to be his true calling and only turned to the oratorio format because of the growing unpopularity of opera. Still, most clergy viewed Handel's works as purely secular and deplored his use of sacred texts. A few years previous, the Bishop of London had caused a big brouhaha over the use of cathedral choristers in a production of *Esther*. Since the only choirs to be had in London were cathedral choirs, the churches could make it impossible for Handel to get enough singers to perform his oratorios. This is why Handel avoided the problem entirely and debuted his masterpiece in Dublin, where he had no such problems.

The Greatest of These Is Charity

As his gift, Handel made sure that all the proceeds from London's annual performance of the *Messiah* were donated to the Foundling Hospital. So helpful was this source of revenue that the Foundling Hospital tried to obtain the exclusive rights to perform the piece after Handel's death, saying that Handel had specified that in his will. Luckily for the rest of us, they failed.

Rise and Shine

The most persistent legend about the *Messiah* is that we stand during the "Hallelujah Chorus" because King George II stood at this point in the first London performance. The story goes that he had fallen asleep and mistakenly thought it was the end of the piece. Well, it's true that the king—and perforce the rest of the audience—stood, but no one can confirm or deny that it was because he'd fallen asleep.

The Test of Time

The *Messiah* has always had famous supporters and detractors. Beethoven was a particular fan, and Mozart wrote his own arrangement of it. On the other hand, Liszt deplored the *Messiah*, and Hector Berlioz declared it "a barrel of roast pork and beer."

The *Messiah* is Handel's most enduring work and has come to represent all that's British, even though its composer was a German expat. Handel had the good fortune of seeing its rise to popularity in his own lifetime. Several portraits and a statue of him created at the time picture Handel resting a hand on a leaf of the *Messiah* score. In fact, the last performance he ever heard was the *Messiah*.

Twenty-seven may be too much of a good thing when it comes to playing Christmas songs on the radio. One disc jockey was fired for playing "Grandma Got Run Over By a Reindeer" in a row one time too many. Of course, it wasn't all his fault—each repeat was by request.

Huge for the Holidays

The holder of four Guinness World Records, Sergio Rodriguez Villarreal is in a class by himself when it comes to oversized Christmas ornaments. This native of Nuevo Leon, Mexico, uses some strange materials (like beer bottles, plastic cups, and galvanized steel) to create the biggest holiday decorations around.

The Biggest Bell

In 2000, Villarreal assembled this big bell using the glass from 4,854 bottles. The red and white bell stood 18 feet tall and was 12 feet wide at its base.

The Biggest Ball

What's blue and red and green and shiny all over? It's the world's biggest Christmas ball, which measures more than 13 feet in diameter, and lights up both on the inside and outside. Villarreal made this bauble out of galvanized steel and plastics.

The Biggest Angel

Measuring 18 feet high and 11 feet wide, the world's biggest Christmas Angel is tall, silver, and made from 2,946 bottles of beer. She's very shiny, too—that's because each beer bottle still has its metal cap on tight.

The Biggest Wreath

In 1997, Villarreal created a huge Christmas wreath out of 5,983 disposable plastic cups. At its widest point, it measured more than 10 feet across.

What's in a Name?

The gift-bringer at Christmastime goes by a variety of names throughout the world. Here are just a few:

Christkindl — Austria, Germany, Switzerland
Father Christmas — England
Grandfather Frost — Russia
Hoteiosho — Japan
Joulupukki — Finland
Julemanden — Denmark
Père Noël — France
Saint Nicholas — Belgium, the Netherlands
Swiety Mikolaj — Poland
Three Kings — Spain, Mexico

A Town Called Christmas

For most of us, Christmas comes once a year, but what do you do when you live in a place called Christmas? Or Santa Claus? Let's take a quick tour of some of the U.S. towns that have the holiday spirit all year long.

Christmas, Michigan

This town on Michigan's Upper Peninsula was founded fairly recently: 1938, when one Julius Thorson got the bright idea of building a factory that made holiday gifts—and what could be more irresistible than holiday gifts from Christmas? Alas for Mr. Thorson, the factory burned down in 1940. But the town survived and gained its first post office in 1966, and the post office now offers its postmark for all comers. Aside from the expected Christmas-oriented mall filled with ornaments, gifts, and other seasonal goodies, Christmas is also home to Kewadin's Christmas casino, so you can double down on all that holiday cash.

Christmas, Florida

Why should snowbound climes have all the fun? This town, some 25 miles east of Orlando, was the site of Fort

Christmas, founded on Christmas Day, 1837, when 2,000 or so U.S. troops and Alabama volunteers built a supply depot for use in the Second Seminole War. The fort was abandoned in 1838 and later destroyed in a forest fire, but a replica was reconstructed in 1977, and the road to the new fort is marked—naturally enough—with a Christmas tree. As with its Michigan counterpart, the postmark for this town is a popular one.

Santa Claus, Indiana

Local legend has it that this little burg got its name on Christmas Eve of 1852. Seems that the settlers of the town were having a hard time agreeing on a name for their new town. They were arguing about it after Christmas Eve services, when the doors to the church blew open, and jingle bells were heard. The children exclaimed, "It's Santa Claus!" and suddenly the settlers had the name for their town. Well, it's a nice local legend.

Santa Claus naturally has a number of Santa-related attractions, from the 22-foot-high, 40-ton granite statue of Santa, to the Holiday World and Splashin' Safari amusement parks (which got their start as Santa Claus Land) that claims to have the world's best wooden roller coaster. Santa would be proud. And yes, you can get a postmark here, too.

Frankenmuth, Michigan

Even though the name of this town doesn't sound very Christmasy, it gets its Christmas association thanks to Bronner's, which boasts of being the world's largest year-round Christmas store. And before you say, "Yeah, but what's the competition?" let us flood you with trivia: The Bronner's compound covers 27 acres, has 7.35 acres of actual buildings, and lights up over 100,000 Christmas lights every night, which is why Bronner's reports having an electric bill of more than $900 a day. So, it's not just an idle claim—the place has the Christmas shtick down cold, which may possibly be why Bronner's Christmas Wonderland claims 2 million visitors a year.

According to the National Christmas Tree Association, 7 out of 10 Christmas trees displayed in the United States in 2003 were artificial.

Arguably one of the oddest sights in the history of sports takes place in Newtown, Wales, every December. More than 2,500 runners—both male and female—participate in a four-mile race for charity . . . all dressed in full Santa Claus garb: black boots, red pants, red coat, and big white beard.

The Twelve Ornaments of Christmas

The secret to a good marriage? Christmas ornaments, of course. According to a Bavarian custom called the "Bride's Tree," there are 12 special molded glass ornaments that newlyweds need to hang on their tree. Each one reminds them of what's necessary for a successful relationship.

Angel (God's Guidance)
Bird (Joy)
Fish (Christ's Blessing)
Flower Basket (Good Wishes)
Fruit Basket (Generosity)
Heart (True Love)
House (Protection)
Pine Cone (Fruitfulness)
Rabbit (Hope)
Rose (Affection)
Santa (Good Will)
Teapot (Hospitality)

A George Lucas Christmas

A Christmas sci-fi special you have to see—if you can get your hands on it. This story was originally told in Uncle John's Slightly Irregular Bathroom Reader.

Released in May 1977, *Star Wars* was one of the highest-grossing movies of all time. Still, the producers were worried. The sequel wouldn't come out for three more years. How could they make sure fans wouldn't lose interest?

Director George Lucas came up with an idea: *The Star Wars Holiday Special,* a two-hour TV show to air near Thanksgiving 1978. Lucas wrote a story about how the *Star Wars* characters celebrated Christmas, or Life Day, as they called it. The plot would follow Chewbacca's family as they awaited his return home for the holiday. Meanwhile, Han Solo and Chewbacca would be delayed trying to thwart Darth Vader's plan to ruin Life Day for the entire universe. They'd fight him off and make it home to Wookiee world just in time.

The Saga Begins

Lucas sold the idea to ABC, and it looked like the show might be pretty good. Almost all the original cast agreed to appear. The production team behind *Star Wars* was on board for special effects and makeup. Advertisements promised never-before-seen action sequences of Han Solo and Chewbacca flying through space fighting Darth Vader's spaceships. It might have been a Christmas classic, but by the time production began, Lucas was busy with the early stages of *The Empire Strikes Back,* and ABC left the special in the hands of a team of novice staff writers.

The Mediocre Strikes Back

The Star Wars Holiday Special aired at 8:00 p.m. on November 17, 1978. All expectations instantly evaporated during the first 15 minutes, which consisted of Chewbacca's family arguing in Wookiee language—without subtitles. That foreshadowed the rest of the program: a tacky variety show with a *Star Wars* theme. It had no plot. It mostly showed Chewbacca's whining, grunting relatives watching 3-D television, with sequences that included Beatrice Arthur in an off-key song-and-dance number; a virtual reality erotic dance from Diahann Carroll; a performance of "Light the Sky on Fire" by Jefferson Starship; and a cooking show with a six-armed Harvey Korman in drag. It all concluded with a Life Day carol sung by Princess Leia—to the tune of the *Star Wars* theme song. (Actress Carrie Fisher later confessed that she was "highly medicated" during filming.) As the show progressed and each sequence became more outlandish than

the last, most of the 20 million viewers flipped over to
Wonder Woman.

Rebel Fighters

Despite the initially large audience, reviews were awful and
true fans hated it. So did George Lucas. He was furious that
the special had corrupted his beloved characters. Because of
his anger (and his clout), Lucas managed to prevent *The Star
Wars Holiday Special* from ever airing again. He assumed that
the show would be an unfortunate but quickly forgotten mis-
step in his career. But that's not what happened.

In 1978, the prospect of seeing *Star Wars* in your own
home was irresistible, and that year was the beginning of the
VCR revolution. Many viewers taped the show, which set
into motion a vast bootlegging network that widely distrib-
utes this otherwise forgettable flop to this day. Though most
copies are of very poor quality, they can still be obtained
cheaply via the Internet. "If I had the time and a sledgeham-
mer," Lucas once commented, "I would track down every
bootlegged copy of that program and smash it."

❦

"A lovely thing about Christmas is that
it's compulsory, like a thunderstorm,
and we all go through it together."

—*Garrison Keillor, radio personality*

Candy Canes

A few quick facts on the peppermint-flavored treat.

What It Is: A crook-shaped stick of hard, red-and-white striped candy. Often peppermint flavored.

Where It Came From: Candy canes have been around for more than three centuries. They did get their start as a holiday treat—and also as a method of noise control. The story goes that in the 1670s a choirmaster in Cologne, Germany, was annoyed by children making noise during the church's lengthy, living-crèche ceremony. Instead of punishing the chatterboxes, he had these hooked white candies made to keep the kiddies' mouths occupied with eating, rather than talking, during the services.

How It Got on the Tree: Because of the convenient crooked shape (candy canes were shaped to resemble a shepherd's staff), the confection was perfect for hanging on Christmas trees. Germans adopted the practice and it soon spread.

Why It Looks That Way: No one really knows how or when the candy cane first got its stripes. Until the early 20th century, most depictions of the treat show just a plain white stick. Christmas cards and other illustrations started showing the red-and-white version around 1900. Today you can get candy canes in just about any color and flavor you like.

Fun Facts

- Every year, 1.76 billion candy canes are made.
- December 26 is National Candy Cane Day in the United States.
- The biggest candy cane ever made was 36 feet, 7 inches long.
- A medium-size candy cane has about 50 calories.

A Very Special Christmas Episode

The holiday season can be so busy. With all the shopping, cooking, wrapping, and eating, there just isn't time to catch up on all those Christmas episodes of your favorite TV shows. We've done the watching for you, and put together this short list of holiday episodes.

The Brady Bunch

The Title: "The Voice of Christmas" (first aired 12/19/69)

The Plot: Oh, no! Carol (Florence Henderson) is supposed to sing in church on Christmas Day, but then she loses her voice. A job for an ear, nose, and throat specialist? Not according to little Cindy (Susan Olsen), who goes to a higher authority: the department store Santa Claus, whom she asks to bring back her mommy's voice.

Obscure Trivia: When Carol does regain her voice on Christmas morning, she sings "O Come All Ye Faithful."

Friends

The Title: "The One With the Holiday Armadillo" (first aired 12/14/00)

The Plot: Ross (David Schwimmer) tries to interest his

young son Ben (Cole Sprouse) in the Jewish holidays as part of his heritage, but Ben only wants to talk about Santa. Being a good father, Ross tries to find a Santa suit, can't find one, and has to settle for another costume: the Holiday Armadillo. Confusion ensues as Chandler (Matthew Perry) shows up as Santa, then Joey (Matt LeBlanc) appears in a Superman costume. But eventually Santa, Superman, and the Holiday Armadillo get Ben to light Hanukkah candles.
Obscure Trivia: Ross tells his son that the Holiday Armadillo is Santa's representative in the southern United States and Mexico.

Married With Children
The Title: "It's a Bundyful Life" (first aired 12/17/89)
The Plot: With a name like "It's a Bundyful Life," you need to know the plot? Fine: Blue-collar slob Al Bundy (Ed O'Neill) gets a glimpse of what life would be like for everyone he knows if he had never been born. It turns out that his wife Peggy (Katey Sagal) would be able to cook and his kids would be smart. Another twist: The guardian angel in this story is played by loud, late comedian Sam Kinison, your assurance that whatever this episode may be, it ain't no Frank Capra film.
Obscure Trivia: The very first half-hour *Simpsons* appearance also happened that evening: *The Simpsons Christmas Special* (the success of which led to the TV series).

The Honeymooners

The Title: "Honeymooner's Christmas Party" (first aired: 12/12/53)

The Plot: While setting out holiday snacks, Alice Kramden (Audrey Meadows) discovers Ralph (Jackie Gleason) has gotten the wrong potato salad and sends him out to buy the right kind. In his absence a revolving door of characters (all played by Gleason) tromp through the Kramdens' apartment, with much singing, dancing, and telling of stories. Eventually Ralph reappears, having missed all the excitement; he was nabbed by a cop who thought he was trying to break into the store with the potato salad. That Ralph!

Obscure Trivia: For Christmas, Ralph gives Alice a juicer shaped like Napoléon Bonaparte that squirts juice out of its ear.

"I stopped believing in Santa Claus when I was six. Mother took me to see him in a department store and he asked for my autograph."

—*Shirley Temple, entertainer*

Kristine Kringles

Santa's not the only gift bringer. He's got some female counterparts around the world who bring their own flavor to Christmas traditions.

Gryla and the Yule Lads (Iceland)

Though Gryla and her large family of 13 sons (called Yule Lads) are much anticipated by the children of Iceland, Gryla's origins are, admittedly, disturbing. Folklore has this family of cannibalistic ogres terrorizing the countryside each holiday season—with a particular taste for children. Much like Santa's "naughty and nice list," Icelandic parents use the threat of Gryla and her mischievous offspring to help curb their unruly children. Today, the Yule Lads plague the children of Iceland with pranks—by stealing food, slamming doors, peeping in windows, etc.—but they also place little gifts and treats in kids' shoes that have been left on the window sill.

Kolyada (Russia)

Kolyada is a white-robed maiden who travels through Russia on a sleigh, accompanied by carol singers. She goes from house to house leaving gifts for the children. According to legend, she is believed to be both the goddess of winter and the goddess of the sun.

Snow Maiden (Russia)

Snow Maiden (known as Snegurochka) is Grandfather Frost's granddaughter. Young and pretty and dressed in a blue, fur-trimmed costume, she accompanies her grandfather on his rounds delivering gifts and candies to Russian children. Snow Maiden returns every winter. But when spring comes, folklore says she will melt away unless she returns to her snowy home in the North.

Saint Lucia (Norway, Sweden, and Finland)

The Christmas season in Scandinavia begins on December 13, the feast day of Saint Lucia. During the 1st century, Lucia was tortured and put to death when she refused to give up her religion to marry an unbeliever. As her legend spread, she came to be known as the Lucia Bride; she went from house to house giving out gifts and treats, while dressed in white and carrying a candle. Today, the oldest daughter in the family assumes the role of the Lucia Bride for the day.

La Befana (Italy)

According to Italian lore, the Three Wise Men stopped at Befana's house seeking directions to the humble stable and the newborn babe. She had no information to share, and though she was invited to accompany them, Befana begged off with excuses that household chores needed her attention. After the Wise Men left, she immediately regretted her decision and went to find the noblemen, but they had gone without a trace. Now, on the day of Epiphany or the Day of the Wise Men (January 6) she goes out in search of the babe—her arms laden with gifts. Since her search is fruitless, she leaves her gifts instead with little children on her journey.

Baboushka (Russia)

Russia's equivalent to La Befana, the old lady Baboushka is said to have intentionally given the wrong directions to the Three Wise Men when they came to her door in search of the baby Jesus. Repenting of her misdeed, but unable to find the Wise Men to correct it, she now leaves gifts for sleeping children on the eve of Epiphany.

Tante Arie (France)

This elderly gift bringer visits the Franche-Comté region of France at Christmastime. She lives in the mountains and comes down only to leave offerings for kids; good children can expect a gift, but the wicked ones get dunce caps. Children in other parts of France receive gifts from Père Noël, a tall, thin gentleman who dresses very much like Santa Claus.

Classic Movie Quotes

Some movie lines are unforgettable.

"Christmas? Christmas means dinner, dinner means death!
Death means carnage; Christmas means carnage!"

—Ferdinand the Duck, *Babe*

"The best way to spread Christmas cheer is singing loud for
all to hear."

—Buddy, *Elf*

"Merry Christmas, you beautiful old savings and loan! Merry
Christmas, you beautiful beat-up old house!"

—George Bailey, *It's a Wonderful Life*

"Faith is believing in things when common sense tells you
not to."

—Fred Gailey, *Miracle on 34th Street*

"And the Grinch, with his Grinch-feet ice cold in the snow,
stood puzzling and puzzling, how could it be so? It came with-

out ribbons. It came without tags. It came without packages, boxes or bags. And he puzzled and puzzled 'till his puzzler was sore. Then the Grinch thought of something he hadn't before. What if Christmas, he thought, doesn't come from a store. What if Christmas, perhaps, means a little bit more."

—Narrator, *How the Grinch Stole Christmas*

"And it was always said of [Scrooge], that he knew how to keep Christmas well, if any man alive possessed the knowledge. May that be truly said of us, and all of us! And so, as Tiny Tim observed, God bless us, every one!"

—Narrator, *A Christmas Carol*

If you were to shout "Merry Christmas!" to a passing neighbor in the antebellum South on Christmas morning, you may have received a questioning look. The phrase to shout was "Christmas Gift!" In return, your neighbor was supposed to give you a gift.

The 25 Years of Pants

*Take two brothers-in-law and add one pair of unwanted pants.
Then toss in some competitive spirit and a knack for creative packaging. And what do you get? An amazing holiday tradition.*

On Christmas 1964, Larry Kunkel, then a Minnesota
college student, got a present from his mom: a pair of
sturdy, yellow, moleskin pants—that stiffened in the cold
Minnesota winters. After Kunkel discovered that moleskin
pants froze, he decided to bestow them on his brother-in-law,
Roy Collette, as a Christmas gift. Collette didn't care for
them either, so he gave them back to Kunkel the following
year. And so began a glorious tradition in pants swapping
that endured between the two men for many Christmases.

For Me? You Shouldn't Have

For 25 years, Larry Kunkel and Roy Collette devised new
and sneaky ways to stick the other with the pants every
Christmas. The Minnesota brothers-in-law would package
them in a container that was difficult—but not impossible—to open. The pants had to be removed unscathed in
order to qualify for regifting the following year. Every

Christmas, the packaging became more and more elaborate as each man tried to outdo the other. The agreed upon rules: only junk parts could be used for wrapping materials, expenses must be kept to a minimum, and if the pants were damaged the game would end.

Check out some of the ways Kunkel and Collette packaged the moleskin pants.

- a welded shut, 600-pound, green-and-red-striped safe
- an 8 x 2-foot truck tire filled with 6,000 pounds of concrete ("Have a Goodyear!" said the tag)
- a 17$\frac{1}{2}$-foot, 6-ton model rocket filled with concrete
- a green, 3-foot cube that was a compacted 1974 AMC Gremlin (The tag said the pants were in the glove compartment.)
- a 225-pound steel ashtray made from 8-inch steel casings
- a 4-ton replica of a Rubik's Cube
- a station wagon filled with 170 steel generators all welded together

The Demise of the Pants

Just when it was starting to seem as if the pants might outlive their owners, tragedy struck. In 1989, Collette sent the pants away to be encased in 10,000 pounds of glass. But as the molten glass was poured over the moleskin pants, they were incinerated. The pants had finally been destroyed. That Christmas, Collette sent Kunkel a brass urn filled with the ashes of the pants, accompanied by this epitaph: "Sorry Old Man, here lies the pants . . . An attempt to cast the pants in glass brought about the demise of the pants at last."

The legendary Canadian department store, Eaton's, in Toronto, Ontario, started its annual Santa Claus Parade (featuring one float—Santa Claus) in 1905 to attract customers to the store. As it happened, the thousands of people who jammed Toronto's Yonge Street for the parade took their business to an archrival. With Santa installed on the premises, Eaton's was too crowded for comfortable shopping. (Needless to say, the competition loved the parade.) Eaton's kept at it anyway for more than 75 years, retiring from the parade business in 1982.

Radio City's Christmas Spectacular featuring the world-famous Rockettes debuted in 1933 and is an enduring holiday tradition.

A Reindeer Called . . . Rollo?

From Gene Autry to Burl Ives, the little reindeer with the bright red nose has left his mark on Christmas.

Remember the ninth reindeer? He's the misfit reindeer with the bright red nose that lights up against his will—making him feel like he won't ever really belong with Santa and the other reindeers at the North Pole. But that's just what we know from the movie. Uncle John went looking for Rudolph's real story. Here's what he learned.

What's in a Name?

In 1939, Robert May, a copywriter for Montgomery Ward, was asked to write a Christmas poem for the holiday season. May came up with one he called "Rollo the Red-Nosed Reindeer." Executives of the company liked the story, but didn't like the name Rollo. So May renamed the reindeer Reginald—the only name he could think of that preserved the poem's rhythm. Montgomery Ward rejected that name, too. Try as he might, May couldn't come up with another

name that fit—until his four-year-old daughter suggested
Rudolph.

A Little Reindeer Goes a Long Way

The poem was a huge success. Montgomery Ward published
a little book out of it and sold some two and a half million
copies that season. Ten years later, the popular story about the
misfit reindeer was set to music by Robert May's brother-in-
law, songwriter Johnny Marks. When the song was recorded
by singing cowboy Gene Autry, "Rudolph the Red-Nosed
Reindeer" (betcha can hear it now) became the second-best-
selling Christmas single in history—after "White Christmas."

Animagic Effects

But that's just the beginning of the little reindeer's popularity.
Most of us have seen—on a yearly basis perhaps—the classic
Animagic special, *Rudolph the Red-Nosed Reindeer,* which aired
for the first time in 1964 on the *General Electric Fantasy Hour.*
In the show, Yukon Cornelius, Hermey the Elf, and the misfit
toys all help Rudolph save Christmas.

Narrated by Burl Ives, the TV special has been watched by an estimated 100 million families over
the years. Today the show, and
Rudolph, are permanently estab-
lished in the Christmas tradition.

Gifts of Christmas Past:
The 1970s

*From a personal mummy case to mood rings, Christmas gifts during
the Me Decade were innovative and surprising.*

Starting Out Big

The 1971 *Neiman Marcus Christmas Book* kicked off the
decade by offering authentic His and Her sarcophagi from
Ancient Egypt at a mere $6,000 each. Neiman Marcus didn't
realize that one of the decorated coffins contained a real,
2,600-year-old mummy, until a shipping room clerk heard
some rattling inside. The Rosicrucian Egyptian Museum in
California snapped it up, eventually paying $16,000. The
mummy of Usermontu—his name was conveniently
inscribed in hieroglyphics on the sarcophagus—is now a popular exhibit.

If Mummies Weren't Your Bag

Those who balked at spending so much on a Christmas present in the early 1970s had other choices. For him: 2 million
Pocket Fisherman gadgets were sold in the two years after its

1973 introduction. Polyester leisure suits were briefly popular, mainly because the hero of the *Six Million Dollar Man* TV show wore them. For her: Hot pants were in, if you looked like Jackie Onassis or Twiggy. For the rest, try macramé plant hangers holding a new coleus, or the #1 fiction best seller of 1972, *Jonathan Livingston Seagull.*

A Very Good Year

The year 1975 was a memorable year for Christmas gifts. The Sony Betamax with wired remote, priced just under $2,300, hit stores in November. This was the first VCR sold in the United States, or just about anywhere, and it came attached to a 19-inch color TV.

The original Mood Ring (there were countless imitations) cost $19.95, although Neiman Marcus carried a 14-karat gold version for a bit more. Mood rings changed color depending on the emotional state of the wearer (actually, the liquid crystals in the ring changed with skin temperature). Between 15 and 20 million were sold that year.

Video games were first packaged for home use. Through December, people spent hours in lines at 900 Sears stores nationwide to buy Pong. Sears had purchased the distribution rights in 1975, saving Pong's maker, Atari, from bankruptcy.

Digital watches debuted. In 1975, 2.5 million LED and LCD watches were sold, priced anywhere between $30 and $3,000.

A Promising Ending

In 1976, CB radios were popular; First Lady Betty Ford owned one and broadcast under the handle First Mama.

The year 1977 was the Year of the Great Shortage. Buyers were flush with funds, but shelves were nearly empty. Some stores resorted to creative solutions, like selling Cuisinart boxes with a gift certificate inside, instead of the back-ordered food processor. Kenner Products had exclusive rights to *Star Wars* paraphernalia, but was unprepared for the demand. Not wanting to miss an opportunity, they sold IOUs through the Christmas season, redeemable as soon as the movie-inspired toys became available.

Faux Français

In 1977 consumers saw the first designer jeans, manufactured by the Nakash Brothers of New York. Jordache was embroidered over the right rear pocket—the brothers thought it sounded more elegantly French than Nakash—*et* voilà! Trendy was redefined. By 1979, 30 different pocket-names— like Calvin Klein, Sasson, and Sergio—were vying with Sony's new toy, the Walkman portable sound system, for consumer dollars at Christmas.

Christmas confectionery sales total approximately $1.4 billion annually.

Calendar Calculations

Early calendars have Jesus born in A.D. 1, but it looks like the calendars were wrong. We got it straight from Uncle John's Ultimate Bathroom Reader.

A New Beginning

Prior to the 6th century, the European calendar was based on the years counted from the founding of Rome or A.U.C. (anno urbis conditae, or the year of the founding of the city.) In 1288 A.U.C. (A.D. 534), a Ukrainian monk named Dionysius Exiguus decided that the Christian calendar ought to be based on Jesus' birth. Under the patronage of Pope John I, he set out to try to figure exactly when Jesus was born. It was a difficult task: The date of Jesus' birth isn't mentioned anywhere in the Bible. Still, working from vague gospel accounts, official Roman records, and astrological charts, Dionysius eventually settled on 754 A.U.C. as Jesus' birthday. He called it A.D. 1 (for anno Domini, or the year of the Lord).

Reconsidering the Calendar

But what if our Ukrainian monk were wrong? The New

Testament clearly states that King Herod was ruler of Judea at the time of Jesus' birth. Since Herod's death is firmly dated at 4 B.C., Jesus must have been born about that time. (Some argue he may have been born as early as 12 B.C.) If that's the case, the real year 2000 is actually between 2004 and 2020.

The New Millennium, 2001

Furthermore, Dionysius's decision to begin his new calendar with year 1 instead of year 0 meant that by the beginning of year A.D. 2, only one year had elapsed; by A.D. 10, only nine years had passed; and by A.D. 100, only 99 years had been completed. You get the point. Extend this logic to the present day, and you realize that by the year 2000, only 1,999 years have elapsed. So it was the first day of the year 2001, not of 2000, that started the new millennium.

Even knowing this, we'll probably keep the calendar just the way it is. But one thing's clear: Dionysius probably should have left the calendar calculating to the mathematicians of the day.

"From a commercial point of view,
if Christmas did not exist it would be
necessary to invent it."

—*Katharine Whitehorn,*
British journalist

Festivus
for the Rest of Us

Seinfeld, the show about nothing, actually gave us something for the holidays: a new December tradition in which everyone can participate. Here's a little primer on Festivus.

On December 18, 1997, the world was introduced to Festivus, the December holiday for "the rest of us." Occurring on December 23, this simple "celebration" came about after George Costanza's father, Frank, fought a heated physical battle for the last toy in a department store. He invented Festivus when he "realized there had to be a better way," and developed the holiday focused on familial disappointments and feats of strength, instead of materialism. But was that really the origin? The truth of the matter is that the roots of Festivus go back much further. How far back? Thousands of years? Hundreds? Well, no: Try 1966.

Family Traditions
In 1966 Daniel O'Keefe, an editor at *Reader's Digest*, celebrated the anniversary of his first date with his wife, Deborah, and named the party Festivus. Traditions began to

evolve after O'Keefe was inspired by Samuel Beckett's absurdist play *Krapp's Last Tape,* which features an older man listening to tape recordings of his younger self. O'Keefe started making his own tapes, into which he'd record his grievances about life; these tapings became incorporated into Festivus as the O'Keefe family began to record all their complaints, too. In the original O'Keefe family tradition, grievance airings were not tied to any particular day and could occur at any time between December and May. Grievance airings were also offered on dour annual themes such as, "Is there a light at the end of the tunnel?" and "Too easily made glad?" In addition to the tape recordings, there would be wrestling matches between O'Keefe's three sons.

The Seinfeld Connection

Many years later O'Keefe's son, also named Daniel, became a writer for *Seinfeld* and recounted the O'Keefe traditions to his fellow writers. The O'Keefe family traditions formed the cornerstone of the Seinfeldian Festivus.

Ever since the airing of that 1997 *Seinfeld* episode, Festivus has taken on a life of its own. According to the *Seinfeld* tradition, the holiday features three primary elements:

1. The Aluminum Pole: The holiday's only decoration, the stark, unadorned pole symbolizes resistance to the commercialization of the holidays. No tinsel is allowed: Frank Costanza says it's "distracting."

2. The Airing of Grievances: During the Festivus dinner, celebrants go around the table and tell friends and family how they disappointed them over the past year.

3. The Feats of Strength: The head of the family must be wrestled to the ground in order for Festivus to end. The head of the family chooses an opponent; that person must then wrestle the head of the family unless it can be shown that they have something better to do (like, well, pretty much anything).

Another aspect of the holiday is the "Festivus miracle"—a miracle that is only slightly better than no miracle at all: finding 35 cents in your pocket instead of a quarter, for example, or picking up the phone on the fifth ring, just before the caller is about to hang up. Truly, Festivus miracles are all around!

A Life of Its Own

Seinfeld fans, delighted by the absurd holiday, took it for their own. And thus here we are with, as a *New York Times* story put it, "a real holiday made fictional and then real again." Festivus parties have become popular with friends and families across the United States. Many now erect their own aluminum poles. Others have created Festivus greeting cards to list the ways they've been disappointed by others throughout the year.

In 2004, the holiday even moved into the public realm when in Bartow, Florida, a plywood sign stood next to other holiday displays. It read: "Festivus for the Rest of Us. Donated to Polk County by the Seinfeld Fan Club." Some were not amused and aired their grievances to the county commissioners (no word on whether any wrestling took place). But it looks like Festivus is here to stay. So enjoy your aluminum pole, your airing of grievances, and your feats of strength. Happy Festivus!

Want to know what to drink while airing your grievances? Festivus Red might be in order. It's a holiday wine bottled by Oklahoma Winery Grape Ranch and named in honor of the *Seinfeld* holiday.

An Internet search using two telephone databases turned up the following people's names: (1) Feliz Navidad, (1) Merri Christmas, (3) Merry Christmas, (3) Candy Cane, (5) Santa Claus, (16) Mary Christmas. There are also 29 listings for people with the surname Newyear.

A Weed By Any Other Name

Who would have thought a little weed could make such a beautiful difference?

Joel Poinsett, the U.S. ambassador to Mexico in the 1820s, is credited with bringing the poinsettia to the United States in 1828. His prize didn't cause much of a stir. After all, it only had limited cachet in Mexico (the shrub had little more status than a weed south of the border). Back in pre-Columbian days the Aztec people extracted a purplish-red dye from it, presumably for use as a cosmetic. They also reportedly used its latex sap to subdue fevers. Because it bloomed during the Christmas season, Franciscan monks put it to decorative use in Nativity celebrations. Regardless, for centuries there was little ado for the plant.

'Tis The Season

Early in the 20th century, Paul Ecke Sr, a California horticulturalist and marketing genius, transformed Poinsett's colorful weed into wealth. The poinsettia is the number one selling legal weed in America, and the Ecke family descendants still control much of the wholesale market.

A Nontoxic Plant

Poinsettias have no known therapeutic or medicinal qualities other than their ability to heighten Christmas spirits. On the other hand, contrary to urban legend, the plant's leaves and bracts are not poisonous. At least, they didn't hurt the University of Ohio's lab rats when scientists carried out experiments. Scientists have opined that a 50-pound child eating 500 poinsettia flowers would, at worst, have a tummy ache. The same could probably be said of eating any 500 flowers.

Most important, in a salutary move to commemorate Joel Poinsett's death, by an act of Congress, legislators decreed every December 12th to be National Poinsettia Day.

By the Numbers

- Poinsettias come in more than 100 varieties and some 1,400 different colors. Red and pink too common? Try coral, salmon, marble, or champagne.

- Over 60 million poinsettias are sold every Christmas.

- Eighty percent of poinsettias are purchased by women, and 80 percent of purchasers are over 40 years old.

- Annual retail sales of poinsettias now exceed $220 million.

Merry Mondegreens

Getting the words wrong to your favorite songs is called a monde-
green. We asked around, and it seems that even Christmas carols
aren't immune to misinterpretations. Here are some of our favorite
mistakes—the correct lyrics, if you have any doubt, are on the left.

Silent Night

Round yon Virgin, mother and child	Round John Virgin, motherless child
Holy Infant, so tender and mild	Holey lint, sewed tender and mild
Sleep in heavenly peace	Sleep in heavenly peas
Sleep in heavenly peace	Sleep in heavenly peas

Jingle Bells

Bells on bobtail ring	Bells on Bob's tail ring
Making spirits bright	Making spareribs right

Hark the Herald Angels Sing

Peace on Earth and mercy mild	Peace on Earth and mercy mild
God and sinners reconciled	Gold and silver make us smile

Have a Holly Jolly Christmas

Oh, ho the mistletoe	Oh, no the missing toe
Hung where you can see	A hunger you can see

Mall Santas
By the Numbers

*A trip to the mall gives most kids their big chance to see the
oft-elusive Santa Claus. Here are some facts and figures on
the quintessential mall Santa.*

0–3

The age of children who have no interest in meeting Santa—
and they usually cry if they're placed on his lap. By four,
though, they're usually ready to tell him all about their
Christmas wishes.

2

The primary categories in which recruiting companies place
their Santa applicants: Bearded Santas (those with real
whiskers) and synthetic Santas (those who need some whisker
enhancements).

7

The percent of mall Santa applicants with a less than stellar
record. Mall Santas go through an extensive background
check so that those with criminal records are not hired. (Note

that the national average of applicants with criminal records for other jobs is as high as 15 percent.)

45

The percent of mall Santas who are college graduates or who have continued on to graduate school.

50

The number of malls in the United States that give out pagers to parents so they can be beeped when Santa is ready to see their kids. The pager is expected to be used in more and more malls every year.

218

The weight, in pounds, of the average mall Santa.

1,800

The number of U.S. malls that employ a Santa.

1841

The year the first department store, J. W. Parkinson's in Philadelphia, used a life-size Santa (it was just a big stuffed doll in the window) to get parents and kids in the store during the holiday season.

4,600

On average, the amount of kiddie pictures taken with Santa at each mall every holiday season.

10,119

The number of children who visit Santa at each U.S. mall every holiday season.

30,000

Amount in dollars a good mall Santa could make in the six- to eight-week season. Most full-time Santas earn closer to $10,000 for the season.

18,214,200

The total number of kids who visit Santa Claus at all the U.S. malls each Christmas holiday.

Playing Santa at the mall requires some quick thinking; he's got to come up with a reply to even the toughest requests. A kid wants a pet? No problem. "There's no water in the sleigh." How about an expensive toy? Here, Santa's got a couple of options: "When I get to your house I'll check my sleigh for it," or, "I'm working with your parents on this one. We need to talk about it together." After all, Santa needs to remain noncommittal.

An Old Flame

The setting was New York City, a place full of apartments but short on fireplaces. Year in and year out, many New Yorkers had to go without a crackling fire to help celebrate Christmas. That was until 1966, when a television executive came up with a brilliant idea.

Hearth for the Holidays

The general manager of local television station WPIX-Channel 11, Fred M. Thrower, felt for these hearthless people and wanted to help "all the cave dwellers in New York, all the apartments that don't have fireplaces." He came up with the idea of filming and broadcasting a burning Yule log, so everyone could gather round the fireplace—televised or otherwise.

Thrower arranged for the first Yule log to be shot in a hearth at Gracie Mansion, the New York City mayor's official residence. On the set, the crew wanted a clearer view of the blaze and removed a protective screen. They got a great shot, but burning embers damaged a $4,000 rug in the process.

The Yule log aired on that Christmas Eve. With a sound track of Christmas carols, the 17-second, repeating loop of fiery footage mesmerized viewers. The entire three-hour broadcast ran commercial free, a decision that cost the station about the same amount as the damage done to the rug in Gracie Mansion. Over 1 million viewers tuned in to watch the fire that night. Former WPIX vice president Richard N. Hughes remembers Thrower's creation fondly: "His motives were entirely noble in things like this . . . It was so characteristic of the way he operated—that he'd say we're going to take a few hours off and give people a Christmas card."

The successful Yule log telecast quickly became a staple of New York City holiday television with fans all over the tri-state area. Airing on both Christmas Eve and Christmas Day, the televised fire provided a cozy (if artificial) atmosphere by which to open presents, drink eggnog, and celebrate the holiday. Eventually the log soundtrack was simulcast in stereo on WPIX-FM, so the accompanying carols could fill the entire house.

The Flame Dies Down

As the years went by, some of the Yule log's luster began to wear off. The first sign was that the broadcast was cut back to two hours. Then in 1989, the Yule log disappeared from TV screens. WPIX executives felt that the show was too hokey and that the commercial-free format did nothing but burn up money. They extinguished the Yule log in favor of "traditional Christmas programming" (e.g., the kind with commercials).

Residents of the tri-state area would have to do without the televised Christmas fire for 12 dark years.

Dispirited citizens did not take the loss of their log lightly. In 1997, WPIX tried to assuage them by streaming the log on their Web site, but it just wasn't the same thing. Then in February 2001, Joe Malzone of Totowa, New Jersey, decided that he had had enough. He launched a Bring Back the Log Web site to try to resuscitate the holiday tradition. Bring Back the Log touched a nerve; thousands of people wrote to Malzone and shared their memories of the Yule log and expressed how much they missed it. Malzone forwarded their stories to WPIX and hoped for the best.

A Burning Sensation

In 2001, WPIX yielded to popular demand and announced that it would bring back the Yule log that very Christmas. People rejoiced: *New York Post* television critic Linda Stasi wrote, "I really love that darned log, and I've missed it terribly . . . how can you not love anything as absurd as a fire blazing on a TV screen while Christmas songs play constantly in the background? Brilliant!" WPIX general manager Betty Ellen Berlamino said, "This year just seems like the right time to bring back the Yule log. It's a great tradition, and a lot of people love it." WPIX found the old film (reportedly stored in a can labeled "fireplace"), digitally restored it, and aired it for two hours on Christmas morning.

The result? The Yule log smoked the Christmas morning competition, prompting WPIX executives to revive the annual televised tradition. That decision has paid off, too. Every year since then, the Yule log has led the Christmas morning ratings in New York.

Eternal Flame?

The Yule log isn't just for New Yorkers anymore. It's become a nationwide phenomenon: In major U.S. cities like Los Angeles, San Diego, Seattle, Denver, Charlotte, Chicago, the Twin Cities, and Washington, D.C., television stations have all yielded to the Yule log's simple charm and format. And so  have their viewers. Everywhere the Yule log has been broadcast, it's been a huge ratings success, assuring its place as a beloved, American Christmas institution.

Merry Christmas of South Carolina, has a brother named Noel Whyte Christmas and a sister named Carol Christmas.

Cartoon Christmas:
A Triple-Threat Quiz

*Another quiz to see how well you remember the cartoons of
Christmas past.*

Year after year, children rely on cartoon Christmas specials to start stirring up holiday cheer (and to start introducing them to latest toys, via the commercials). To keep mom and dad happy, these jolly animated classics are also jam-packed with stars. Can you match the celebrity voices with the show's title and the character's name?

Match the Stars ... With Their Characters ...

1. Drew Barrymore

2. Jimmy Durante

3. Boris Karloff

4. Joel Grey

5. Jim Backus"

I.   Joshua Trundle, a clock maker

II. The Grinch, a mean old hermit

III. Ebenezer Scrooge, a mean old miser

IV. The Narrator with a big schnoz

V.   Olive, a talking dog

And the Shows

A. *How the Grinch Stole Christmas!*

A Christmas hater disguises himself as Santa Claus to stop the holiday from coming.

B. *Mr. Magoo's Christmas Carol*

On Christmas Eve, a nearsighted miser is visited by three spirits who teach him to change his ways.

C. *Olive, the Other Reindeer*

A dog must outsmart an evil postman to reach the North Pole and replace an injured reindeer.

D. *Frosty the Snowman*

After a magician's hat brings him to life, a snowman must travel north as rising temperatures threaten to melt him.

E. *'Twas the Night Before Christmas*

A mouse family and a human family attempt to appease Santa Claus, who has been offended by a letter in the town's newspaper.

Turn to page 176 for the answers.

"Next to a circus there ain't nothing that packs up and tears out faster than the Christmas spirit."

—*Kin Hubbard, humorist, cartoonist*

Dear Santa Claus

*Every year children around the world send their wish lists
to Santa, but how do they know where to send them?
It seems that Canada and the United Kingdom have
it all figured out.*

The Great White North Pole
Where to Send It: Santa Claus, North Pole, H0H 0H0,
Canada

Can You Expect a Response? Yes. Thanks to four
Canadian postal workers who began answering Santa's letters
in 1974. Much to the credit of these Canadian postal elves,
Canada Post launched an official Santa Letter Writing
Program in 1983. Twenty years later, for Christmas 2004,
they responded to more than 1 million letters and 30,000
e-mails. And the number of volunteer elves has increased to
more than 15,000. Even better, there are specially trained
elves (we also call them psychiatrists) who volunteer during
the holidays to help respond to letters from troubled children.

Fun Fact: In Canada, Santa has the distinction of being
the only individual with a personal postal code. If you look

closely, you can see that his zip code is a string of Hs and zeros that spell out *Ho Ho Ho.*

On Her Majesty's Santa Service
Where to Send It: Santa Claus, Reindeerland, SAN TA1

Can You Expect a Response? Yes, but you've got to follow the rules. Since 1963 the United Kingdom's Royal Mail service has helped facilitate the mail from British children—and children worldwide—to Santa. As long as the letter has proper postage, a return address, and is addressed to Santa Claus in Reindeerland, each child will get an answer from Santa or one of his many royal helpers.

Fun Fact: In 2002 the royal elves answered the 10 millionth letter sent from the kids in the United Kingdom to Santa. That year, Royal Mail also set up a Webcam, so youngsters could watch Santa and his many British elves receive and respond to their mail in real time.

Gifts of Christmas Past: The 1980s

Pseudo-toys and perfumes marked Christmas gifts during the 1980s.

1980

The first celebrity designer perfume debuted: Sophia, endorsed and publicized by sexy Italian actor Sophia Loren.

1981

A Hungarian professor named Rubik invented a colored cube that could be arranged in 43,252,003,274,489,856,000 different ways. That's forty-three and a quarter quintillion. One of these Rubik's Cube puzzles, given by a wife to her husband for Christmas, was listed as grounds for divorce.

1982

Sony debuted the Watchman, a pocket TV with a 2-inch-square picture, retailing at $350. For less generous budgets, the gift du jour was the Deely Bopper—a pair of glittery antennae attached to a plastic headband. Really.

1983

Newsweek's cover featured the season's must-have gift: Cabbage Patch Kids. Doting parents nationwide stood in lines for up to eight hours, entered lotteries, or paid megabucks to get one of these dolls.

1984

A sparkling white glove, à la Michael Jackson, was very in. This was also the year of Madonna's *Like a Virgin,* so lacy bras and bustiers were suddenly a fashion statement—to be worn on the outside, not the inside, of an ensemble. The board game Trivial Pursuit debuted as well.

1985

Teddy Ruxpin came with audio cassettes that told a story, and those tapes included movement codes. The Teddy toys blinked, swayed, and moved their mouths in sync with the story. Some kids loved it; others were creeped out.

1986

Fatherhood, by Bill Cosby, remained a hot item—if you hadn't already bought it as a Father's Day gift. By Christmas, over 2 million hard copies were sold.

Nintendo and Sega slugged it out in a battle of home video game systems that continued into the next century. Game cartridges like Super Mario Brothers and Donkey Kong were big sellers.

1987

Elizabeth Taylor's perfume, Passion, was the scent every woman wanted to wear—and at $25 for a bottle of the eau de toilette, most women could.

1988

Cher jumped into the perfume wars with Uninhibited at a truly uninhibited $175 an ounce. The fragrance was a popular Christmas present, though Chanel No. 5 remained No. 1, and Passion grossed $50 million that year.

1989

Teenage Mutant Ninja Turtles was the top-selling toy, and hundreds of sock emporiums opened in malls across the country. Colorful, crazy socks were everywhere by the holiday season—including Teenage Mutant Ninja Turtle socks.

Also in 1989, Nintendo released its handheld Game Boy, with black-and-white graphics. At $169, Game Boys came packaged with a game designed by Russian mathematician Alexey Pajitnov, and by Christmas afternoon thousands were addicted to Tetris.

"The perfect Christmas gift for a sportscaster, as all fans of sports clichés know, is a scoreless tie."

—*William Safire, columnist*

Is There a Santa Claus?

This heartfelt query was first printed in the New York Sun *in 1897, along with a response from editor Francis P. Church. It proved so popular that it was reprinted every year until the* Sun *went out of business in 1949.*

Dear Editor: I am 8 years old. Some of my little friends say there is no Santa Claus. Papa says, "If you see it in *The Sun*, it's so." Please tell me the truth; is there a Santa Claus?

Virginia O'Hanlon

Virginia, Your little friends are wrong. They have been affected by the skepticism of a skeptical age. They do not believe except they see. They think that nothing can be which is not comprehensible by their little minds. All minds, Virginia, whether they be men's or children's, are little. In this great universe of ours man is a mere insect, an ant, in his intellect, as compared with the boundless world about him, as measured by the intelligence capable of grasping the whole of truth and knowledge.

Yes, Virginia, there is a Santa Claus. He exists as certainly as love and generosity and devotion exist, and you know that they abound and give to your life its highest beauty and joy.

Alas! How dreary would be the world if there were no Santa Claus! It would be as dreary as if there were no Virginias. There would be no childlike faith then, no poetry, no romance to make tolerable this existence. We should have no enjoyment, except in sense and sight. The eternal light with which childhood fills the world would be extinguished.

Not believe in Santa Claus! You might as well not believe in fairies! You might get your papa to hire men to watch in all the chimneys on Christmas Eve to catch Santa Claus, but even if they did not see Santa Claus coming down, what would that prove? Nobody sees Santa Claus, but that is no sign that there is no Santa Claus. The most real things in the world are those that neither children nor men can see. Did you ever see fairies dancing on the lawn? Of course not, but that's no proof that they are not there. Nobody can conceive or imagine all the wonders there are unseen and unseeable in the world.

You may tear apart the baby's rattle and see what makes the noise inside, but there is a veil covering the unseen world which not the strongest man, nor even the united strength of all the strongest men that ever lived, could tear apart. Only faith, fancy, poetry, love, romance, can push aside that curtain and view and picture the supernal beauty and glory beyond. Is it all real? Ah, Virginia, in all this world there is nothing else real and abiding.

No Santa Claus! Thank God! he lives and lives forever. A thousand years from now, Virginia, nay 10 times 10,000 years from now, he will continue to make glad the heart of childhood.

Christmas in a Nutshell

Starting in late November, The Nutcracker Suite *is everywhere: piped into elevators, on the radio, on TV, on cell phones—the onslaught is inescapable. It's hard to believe, but when it first debuted, critics and audiences alike predicted a quick descent into obscurity. Tchaikovsky would be shocked to see the institution it has become today.*

A Shaky Start

Pyotr Tchaikovsky loved composing ballets, but because his two previous excursions, *Swan Lake* and *Sleeping Beauty,* had not been enthusiastically received, he was reluctant to pen another. When the director of the Imperial Theater in Moscow approached him and choreographer Marius Petipa with the idea of basing a ballet on E. T. A. Hoffman's *The Nutcracker and the Mouse-King,* Tchaikovsky and Petipa balked at the idea. The dark children's story didn't really scream "ballet" to either of them. They both thought the narrative wasn't coherent enough (a charge still lobbed at the ballet today), and there was no part suitable for the prima ballerina.

Tchaikovsky finally agreed to the project when a commission for a one-act opera, *Iolanthe,* was thrown in to sweeten

the deal. To fix the story problems, Petipa decided to use an adaptation of Hoffman's story, streamlined into today's familiar tale: A young girl receives an enchanted nutcracker doll for Christmas, defeats the wicked Mouse King, and travels with the transformed Nutcracker Prince to the Land of Sweets. The whole second act would take place in the enchanted land and be structured around a series of dances (called divertissements) by the sweets. Petipa also created the role of the Sugarplum Fairy for his prima ballerina. It seemed their problems were solved.

Two Thumbs Down

The ballet debuted on December 17, 1892, at the Maryinsky Theatre, as part of an illogical double bill; first the audience watched *Iolanthe*, an exceedingly grim opera, followed by the light-hearted *Nutcracker*. Perhaps it because of the mismatched lineup, but critics hated *The Nutcracker*.

One critic called the new ballet "absurd in conception and execution," and said it would "please only the most uncultured spectators." Other critics turned their noses up at the number of children onstage, especially during the chaotic battle scene. Another critic called the first Sugar-Plum Fairy "corpulent" and "podgy." It was an inauspicious start for the ballet, and another blow to Tchaikovsky. He died less than a year after the ballet flopped. *The Nutcracker*, however, remained in the Maryinsky's active repertoire for 37 years and was performed by a few other Russian companies, but it was never very popular.

Coming to America

The Nutcracker would eventually find lasting fame and fortune in the United States. Most Americans' first exposure to the ballet's music was in Disney's 1940 animated film, *Fantasia*, as fairies, mushrooms, and thistles pranced to the music of "The Nutcracker Suite." Although *Fantasia* was not a box office smash, it did acquaint a lot of the American public with the music and primed them for the ballet.

The first full American performance of *The Nutcracker* was in San Francisco in 1944. Choreographer William

Christensen sought out the advice of George Balanchine, an expatriate Russian who had danced in *The Nutcracker* in Russia as a youth. The ballet caught on in San Francisco and became an annual tradition there.

Based on Christensen's success, Balanchine chose *The Nutcracker* for his first full-length production as choreographer for the New York City Ballet. Using bits of the original choreography, Balanchine reenvisioned the ballet with a sense of childlike wonder. His production premiered on February 2, 1954, to rave reviews. But the ballet's popularity really took off when CBS broadcast it on Christmas night in 1957 and 1958. June Lockhart (of TV's *Lassie*) provided a voice-over narration so children in the audience could follow the story.

After Balanchine's success, there was a *Nutcracker* every place there was a dance studio. Many choreographers tried their best to duplicate Balanchine's choreography, but some tried to be completely different. Regardless of the approach, American audiences flocked to see the ballet. Its Russian pedigree meant that parents across the country could tell themselves that seeing *The Nutcracker* gave their children a bit of culture. For better or worse, it spread and became an American phenomenon.

The Ballet Some Love to Hate

As with anything wildly popular, *The Nutcracker* developed

its share of detractors. They often criticize its bourgeois depiction of family, its army of cute children, and its second act, bursting with dancing sweets but rather short on plot. Because an annual production of *The Nutcracker* keeps many ballet companies afloat financially (it can bring in as much as a third of a company's annual income), *Nutcracker*-haters will just have to endure the seasonal onslaught. The popularity and profitability of the ballet ensures that there'll be visions of Sugar-Plum Fairies for many years to come, or as critic Richard Buckle famously put it, "every Christmas we are all one 'Nutcracker' closer to death."

Modern-day *Nutcracker* detractors like to claim that Tchaikovsky himself hated *The Nutcracker,* but that just ain't so. It is true that while working on the ballet, he did write to a nephew, "This ballet is far weaker than 'The Sleeping Beauty'—no doubt about it." When he finished the score, he even called it "all ugliness." But the composer eventually grew to like his creation and wrote, "Strange that when I was composing the ballet I kept thinking that it wasn't very good, but that I would show them what I can do when I began the opera. And now it seems that the ballet is good and the opera not so good."

Test Your Christmas IQ

*Grab a pencil for this fun little quiz about all sorts of
Christmas trivia.*

1. How many times is Santa Claus mentioned in Clement
Moore's poem "The Night Before Christmas?"
   A. One
   B. Three
   C. Six
   D. None

2. What U.S. state was the last to declare Christmas an offi-
cial holiday?
   A. Texas
   B. Oklahoma
   C. New York
   D. Arkansas

3. Who introduced the Advent calendar to Canada in the 1700s?

    A. Dr. Seuss

    B. Sir John A. Macdonald (Canada's first prime minister)

    C. Martin Luther

    D. German settlers

4. According to a survey of mall Santas, what is the most common question kids ask Santa?

    A. "Why are there other Santas at other malls?"

    B. "Where's the bathroom?"

    C. "Why are candy canes striped?"

    D. "Does that elf ride on the sleigh with you?"

5. What U.S. magazine played a major role in creating the modern image of Santa Claus in the late 1800s?

    A. *Harper's Weekly*

    B. *Cosmopolitan*

    C. *The Saturday Evening Post*

    D. *New Yorker*

6. Which vocal artist first recorded "Rudolph the Red-Nosed Reindeer?"

    A. Frank Sinatra

    B. Danny Kaye

    C. Gene Autry

    D. Burl Ives

7. Which Roman leader is credited with standardizing December 25 as Christmas Day?

    A. Constantine (The Great)

    B. Julius Caesar

    C. Nero

    D. Titus

8. What ancient civilization began the wreath tradition?

    A. Greek

    B. Sumerian

    C. Hun

    D. Roman

9. In what country are children allowed to see Santa delivering their presents?

    A. Canada

    B. Finland

    C. Australia

    D. Hungary

Turn to page 177 for the answers.

"Christmas is a race to see
which gives out first—your money
or your feet."

—*Unknown*

The Pageant of Peace

Lighting the National Christmas Tree, which stands on the Ellipse south of the White House, has been a Washington, D.C. tradition for decades. For a handful of years, the ceremony has been particularly noteworthy.

1923 Calvin Coolidge lit the first National Christmas Tree.

1941 Franklin D. Roosevelt appeared with Prime Minister Winston Churchill for the tree-lighting ceremony, and they both addressed the crowd. To conserve electricity, chimes were used instead of lights. This continued for the duration of World War II.

1946 The lighting ceremony, performed by Harry S Truman, was televised for the first time.

1963 Lighting of the National Christmas Tree was postponed until the 30-day mourning period had passed for the assassination of John F. Kennedy. It was lit on December 22.

1973 Display of the crèche was discontinued following the Supreme Court's ruling on religious freedom.

1979 The tree was not fully lit during the Iran hostage crisis. Only the top ornament on the tree and the 50 surrounding trees, representing each state in the United States, were lit.

1980 The tree was only lit for 417 seconds—one second for every day the hostages had been in captivity. When the hostages were released a few weeks later (on Ronald Reagan's Inauguration Day, January 20, 1981), the tree was lit in their honor.

1981 Ronald Reagan lit the tree this year from the security of the White House. Recent assassination attempts had necessitated the move.

1984 The crèche was reinstated for the Pageant of Peace after 11 years. That year, temperatures above 70 degrees made it the warmest tree-lighting ceremony in history.

1985 Reindeer that had appeared in the pageant since 1959—in commemoration of the statehood of Alaska—were not included in the pageant to appease animal rights activists.

1991 Special guests of this tree-lighting ceremony included Terry Anderson, a 7-year hostage in Lebanon who had been released only days earlier.

2001 Two children of victims of the September 11 terrorist attack on the Pentagon helped light the tree this year.

It's Beginning to Sound a Lot Like Christmas

Some people may be unaware that Uncle John has been keeping a list. And he's checked it twice (several times in fact) to assemble this list of holiday songs to tickle your funny bone.

Grandma Got Run Over by a Reindeer

This song, first played on the radio in 1979, is now the most requested Christmas song ever and has sold more than 10 million copies—despite its macabre subject matter. Performed by Dr. Elmo and Patsy Shropshire and written by Randy Brooks, it's loved and hated by many. "Grandma's" music video put it on the Yuletide map when MTV first placed it into heavy rotation in 1983—despite protests from various seniors' organizations who argued that Grandma's death was no laughing matter. Although some polls have found this to be one of the most hated Christmas songs of all time, "Grandma's" popularity can't be denied. The song has spawned its own animated special, sold more than 1.5 million musical stuffed toys, and made the top five in 2004 on the newest music charts: cell phone ringtone downloads.

Nuttin' for Christmas

This 1955 hit was written by Sid Tepper and Roy C.
Bennett and recorded by six-year-old Barry Gordon. A veri-
table laundry list of everything this kid did wrong through
the year (like putting a tack on his teacher's chair and filling
the sugar bowl with ants), the song's lyrics explain how he's
not expecting any presents this year "cause I ain't been nuttin' but bad." For such a poorly behaved child, he has such
reasonable expectations!

The Twelve Days of Christmas

Featured on the Canadian album *Great White North* is a ren-
dition of this holiday classic by Bob and Doug McKenzie
(better known as Rick Moranis and Dave Thomas). But
instead of the usual partridge and swimming swans, the
McKenzie brothers offer the song up with a Canadian twist.
One the first day of Christmas, they don't receive a partridge
in a pear tree; their true love gives them a "beer . . . in a
tree." Two turtledoves become two turtlenecks. Three French
hens? Bob and Doug get three French toasts. Curious about
the rest? You'll just have to give this one a listen, eh?

I Saw Mommy Kissing Santa Claus

Written by Tommie Connor, this cute song was sung in 1952
by 12-year-old Jimmy Boyd. At the time, many radio stations
thought the song was too risqué and refused to play it, even

though the innocent joke was that the child doesn't realize it's just Daddy dressed up like Santa. But when the youngster sings about what a "laugh" it would be if Daddy walked in on Mommy kissing a fat, jolly, old man who isn't her husband, we can kind of see the radio stations' point. We don't know many Daddies who would find that very funny.

Please Daddy (Don't Get Drunk This Christmas)

Who knew that John Denver was behind one of the most dysfunctional holiday tunes ever strummed on a guitar? Singing from the point of view of an eight-year-old, Denver reminisces about last Christmas when Daddy drank too much and fell down underneath the Christmas tree, much to Mommy's dismay. He asks Daddy to show some restraint this year because he doesn't "want to see my Momma cry." The song reminds us that holiday memories aren't necessarily the happiest ones.

Christmas Don't Be Late

Better known as "The Chipmunk Song," this squeaky song was actually the brainchild of Ross Bagdasarian, the producer of such other novelty favorites as "Come On-a My House" and "The Witch Doctor." Bagdasarian sang all parts: the chipmunks (Alvin, Simon, and Theodore, who were named for executives at Liberty Records) and their manager David

Seville (Bagdasarian's voice at regular speed). "Christmas Don't Be Late" won a Grammy, sold 5 million copies in 1958, and reportedly kept Liberty Records in business. So who are we to keep them off our list? Don't you agree, Alvin? Alvin? ALVINNNNN!

Walkin' Round in Women's Underwear

This song is a parody of "Winter Wonderland," recorded by Bob Rivers and Twisted Radio in 1993. It tells of a man who will be getting nuttin' for Christmas either—that's if he gets caught—since he's borrowing his wife's unmentionables without asking, not that the asking part makes a difference. Memorable lyrics: "Later on / If you wanna / We can dress / like Madonna / Put on some eyeshade / and join the parade / Walking round in women's underwear."

All I Want for Christmas (Is My Two Front Teeth)

The King of Corn, Spike Jones, wins a spot on the list with this song written by Donald Gardner. Jones convinced George Rock, his orchestra's trumpet player, to lisp his way through the song like a little boy. Rock did such a good job that we almost believe there is some kid out there who would be satisfied with only two teeth on Christmas morning. The song caught the attention of the American people and, in 1948, hit #1 on the Hit Parade, staying there for eight weeks.

You Say It's Your Birthday

Birthdays that fall on December 25 are on the Sagittarius-Capricorn cusp, when the sun transitions from Sagittarius to Capricorn. According to astrologer Gary Goldschneider, those born on this day are "achievement oriented" and "bold," but need to be wary of being too "sensationalistic" and "reckless."

December 25, 1642
Future physicist and mathematician, Sir Isaac Newton was born in Lincolnshire, England.

December 25, 1821
Clara Barton, founder of the American Red Cross, was born in Oxford, Massachusetts.

December 25, 1883
Believe it or not! R. L. Ripley was born in Santa Rosa, California.

December 25, 1884
Mr. Layne Hall's claim to fame? When he died in November

1990 at 105, he still had a valid driver's license, making him the world's oldest driver.

December 25, 1887

Conrad Hilton, hotel magnate, was born in San Antonio, New Mexico.

December 25, 1899

Here's looking at you, kid. Humphrey Bogart was born in New York City, New York.

December 25, 1907

Hi-de-hi-de-hi-de-ho! Cab Calloway, musician and bandleader, was born in Rochester, New York.

December 25, 1924

The Twilight Zone's Rod Serling first entered a dimension of sight and sound in Syracuse, New York.

December 25, 1946

Long before "Margaritaville," Jimmy Buffett made his debut in Pascagoula, Mississippi.

December 25, 1958

A baseball superstar with the record for most stolen bases, Rickey Henderson was born in Chicago, Illinois.

Kitschy Christmas

Why do we love those tacky gifts that appear or reappear every holiday season? Pet Rock creator Gary Dahl told People *magazine: "We've packaged a sense of humor." No doubt about it, they definitely make us laugh. Uncle John even wagers that you've given or received one of the following over the years.*

Rock and Roll With It

Want a low-maintenance pet? Rocks are quiet, neat, undemanding, and loyal. In 1975, Gary Dahl, an adman from California, introduced the Pet Rock—complete with official training manual, nesting straw, and cardboard pet carrier with air holes. (You wouldn't want those sweet little rocks to suffocate, would you?) At $3.95 each, Pet Rocks were the must-have gift for the holiday season. Dahl pocketed 95 cents for each one of the 1.3 million authentic Pet Rocks sold (there were cheap imitations) and walked away a rich man. By Memorial Day of 1976, the rocks were being traded for dimes at garage sales.

Ch-Ch-Ch-Ka-Ching

Chia Pets proved more durable. They are a bit more labor-intensive than rocks (you have to seed and water them), but they respond to loving care in a way rocks never could. They grow. And the jingle "Ch-Ch-Ch-Chia" quickly became a Christmas standard.

Millions have been sold, starting with the Chia Ram in 1982. Dinosaurs, Looney Tunes characters, and Shrek and Donkey have been models for the plants. Chia Pets have even made appearances in movies and TV shows.

Here's some trivia for you: Chia plants are related to watercress and were cultivated by early Americans as a high energy food. For years the clay pots were handmade in Central America. (Today, they're still made by hand, but in China.)

Clap On, Clap Off

Joseph Enterprises, the same company that brought us the Chia Pet, also produces another nostalgic Christmas gift: the Clapper. Now there's a jingle everyone recognizes: "Clap on (clap, clap), clap off (clap, clap)!"

It seemed like magic when it debuted in 1984. The Clapper plugged into an outlet, and two other appliances plugged into the Clapper. Remote controls, dimmers, and cable TV pretty much render this gift obsolete, but it still sells—often as a gag.

Old Newsboys Make Goodfellows

Extra! Extra! Read all about it! Charity Cheers Children! Goodfellows Give Great Gifts! No Kiddie Without a Christmas!

People's minds often turn to charity and gift giving during the holiday season, and Detroit businessman James Brady was certainly no exception. In December 1914, Brady saw a cartoon in the *Detroit News* that touched him. Entitled "The Boy He Used to Be," the illustration showed a man balancing a stack of Christmas bundles with one arm and holding the hand of a small, disheveled newsboy with the other. Reminded of his own childhood spent hawking newspapers after his father died, Brady thought that maybe he could help the less-fortunate kids of Detroit have a brighter Christmas. How? Through newspapers.

Brady contacted his friend, *Detroit News* managing editor E. J. Pipp, and the two men came up with a great idea that would enlist the help of the Detroit Newsboys Association. This organization, founded in 1885, consisted of former newsboys who had gone on to great financial success in life.

Brady and Pipp decided that the Old Newsboys would band together for one day a year, take up their former posts on street corners, and sell a special edition of the newspaper to raise money to make sure there was "No Kiddie Without a Christmas." That first year was a success. The Old Newsboys raised more than $2,000 for presents to be delivered to needy children on Christmas morning. The idea caught on, and an annual tradition was born.

My, How You've Grown!

Almost a century later, the Old Newsboys' Goodfellow Fund of Detroit has gone from raising thousands to raising millions for Detroit's children. The annual fundraising effort is carried out much the same way it was in 1914. Now more than 300 volunteers— former newsboys and newsgirls, known as Detroit Goodfellows, as well as police and firefighters—sell Goodfellow Editions of the *Detroit News* and the *Detroit Free Press* on the city's street corners. The price of a paper? "Anything you care to pay." Since the Old Newsboys members pick up administrative costs, all of the proceeds go to the kids' Christmas packages.

The annual fund raiser benefits thousands of children between the ages of 5 and 13 in the Detroit area. Kids not only receive packages filled with toys, books, games, candy, and warm clothes (including shoes, socks, and underwear—it seems no one can escape from them at Christmas) but also benefit programs such as dental care, college scholarships, and trips to summer camp.

In honor of Brady's goodwill that continues to influence the lives of countless children, a monument was erected following his death in 1928. It still stands on Central Avenue as a testament to the original Goodfellow.

Christmas Trivia

- The tradition of sending Christmas cards originated in England in 1843.

- The average American household sends 28 Christmas cards each year.

- China is the leading exporter of Christmas ornaments.

- On average, it takes the American credit card–user six months to pay off his or her holiday bills.

The Christmas of Kiddom

The comedy A Christmas Story *(1983), based on Jean Shepherd's* In God We Trust, All Others Pay Cash, *tells of young Ralph Parker's quest for a BB gun for Christmas. Shepherd plays the narrator, a grown-up Ralph whose voiceover offers a nostalgic, funny, and (somewhat) cynical look back at key moments of his childhood Christmas.*

What Do You Want for Christmas?

Young Ralphie: "I want an official Red Ryder, carbine action, 200-shot range model air rifle!"

Mother: "No, you'll shoot your eye out."

The Narrator: "It was the classic mother–BB gun block: 'You'll shoot your eye out.' That deadly phrase uttered many times before by hundreds of mothers, was not surmountable by any means known to kiddom."

Believing in Santa Claus

The Narrator: "Let's face it, most of us are scoffers. But moments before zero hour, it did not pay to take chances."

Going to See Santa

The Narrator: "The line waiting to see Santa Claus stretched all the way back to Terre Haute. And I was at the end of it."

Christmas Morning

The Narrator: "Christmas had finally come—officially. We plunged into the cornucopia quivering with desire and the ecstasy of unbridled avarice."

Christmas Dinner Goes Wrong

The Narrator: "The heavenly aroma still hung heavy in the house, but it was gone, all gone! No turkey! No turkey sandwiches, no turkey salad, no turkey gravy, turkey hash, turkey à la king, or gallons of turkey soup! Gone, all gone!"

Ralphie Gets His Wish

The Narrator: "Next to me in the blackness lay my oiled, blue-steel beauty. The greatest Christmas gift I had ever received, or would ever receive. Gradually, I drifted off to sleep, pinging ducks on the wing and getting off spectacular hip shots."

A serious fan of the movie, Brian Jones of San Diego couldn't resist paying $150,000 for the Cleveland home where *A Christmas Story* was filmed. In 2005, he learned that eBay was auctioning the four-bedroom house and successfully bid on it. Jones hopes to open a museum and gift shop at the site.

All My Scrooges

Charles Dickens's A Christmas Carol *has been a staple of movies and television for about as long as there have been movies. The first film adaptation came out in 1908, and studios are still churning them out. So which is the Ebenezer Scrooge to watch? Here are just a few of our favorites.*

Alastair Sim (*Scrooge*, 1951)

Sim's Scrooge is widely regarded as the Scrooge against which all other Scrooges must be measured. Why? In addition to the movie's being a very faithful adaptation of Dickens's story, Sim's transition from the cold, implacable miser to the cheerfully reformed (and somewhat manic) survivor at the end (hope we're not giving anything away here) is remarkable. The actor really digs into each emotion Scrooge has and chews it for all it's worth. Movie critic Roger Ebert thinks this version is the best, as does Leonard Maltin, who also ranks Sim's transformation as one of his "favorite scenes of any movie ever."

Albert Finney (*Scrooge*, 1970)

Finney made our list for two reasons. First, he's one of the youngest (he was just 34 when he took the role—which made him 12 years younger than Michael Medwin, who played Scrooge's nephew). Second, he sings. Yes, this Scrooge is a musical, with songs by Leslie Bricusse. Some say that the songs have not aged as well as Finney's fine (and hammy) performance. Keep an eye out for the great Alec Guinness as Jacob Marley, too.

Henry Winkler (*An American Christmas Carol*, 1979)

At the height of his *Happy Days* fame, Henry "the Fonz" Winkler played the Scrooge character (renamed Benedict Slade) in this update. This time, the Yuletide action takes place during the Depression in the United States. Slade, a cold, New England industrialist, repossesses items from the poor on Christmas Eve before he is visited by the three ghosts of Christmas. The new setting works, although the disco-playing, gold chain–wearing Ghost of Christmas Yet to Come is a little distracting.

George C. Scott (*A Christmas Carol*, 1984)

Some maintain that the best Scrooge is George C. Scott in this made-for-TV adaptation, and it's not a bad argument. Scott is jowly, cranky, and imperious in his Scroogery. Plus, Scott's bulkiness makes him the one Scrooge you suspect could beat off ruffians, orphans, and charity solicitors with his cane. This production is lavish and handsome (especially for 1980s TV) and is one of the most-watched versions of the tale.

Bill Murray (*Scrooged*, 1988)

This Scrooge isn't named Scrooge—he's TV network president Frank Cross, and when he's not being visited by the three ghosts of Christmas, he's presiding over a live broadcast version of *A Christmas Carol,* starring Buddy Hackett as Scrooge. Opinions are divided on Murray's performance in this film, but his seemingly improvised final speech has a lot of heart. And this is one of the few *Christmas Carol* variations that you'll laugh most of the way through.

Patrick Stewart (*A Christmas Carol,* 1999)

It's a safe bet to say that this is the favorite version of many *Star Trek* fans. In addition to playing Captain Jean-Luc Picard of the Starship *Enterprise,* Stewart regularly performed a one-man live stage version of *A Christmas Carol* before he was tapped to appear in this 1999 film version, making him one of the most experienced Scrooges out there. Surrounded by a full cast, Stewart shows his affection for the crusty character, and his performance of Scrooge's happy transformation on Christmas morning is one of the best around.

Eat, Drink, and Be Merry . . . or Else

Having a good time at Christmas can bring good (and bad) fortune to your door if you're not careful. To be safe, we've got the guide to staying lucky during the holidays.

Eating

What would Christmas be without dessert? Incomplete and unlucky, that's what. In the United Kingdom, there are a number of sweets with a long list of do's and don'ts, to bring in the good luck and avoid the bad.

Mince pie (filled with fruit, spices, nuts, meat, and alcohol):

- To avoid bad luck, never cut a mince pie. It's recommended that you use your hands.

- For good luck, if someone offers you a mince pie, say yes.

- For each mince pie you eat during the 12 days of Christmas, you'll have one happy month in the new year.

Drinking

Communal drinking of alcohol has played a key role in holiday cheer for a long time. This ritual has its roots in the wassail, which could occur anytime between Christmas Eve and Twelfth Night (January 6). Family, friends, and neighbors would gather to drink toasts from a common bowl of spiced wine or ale. In some cases, wassails were accompanied by bonfires and the shooting of guns. The purpose of the tradition is to bring good fortune, of course!

Being Merry

Even people who rarely raise their voices in song tend to make exceptions at Christmastime. The tradition of singing Christmas carols arose in Europe during the 12th century when traveling players would act out Bible stories. Protestant Reformers cast a chill over caroling (and Christmas fun in general) in England and the colonies during the 17th and 18th centuries. But the tradition came back in the 19th century during the Victorian era, when revelers were known to knock on doors and demand a drink. If carolers stop by your home, consider this advice to keep your luck intact. Invite carolers into your house and never send them away empty-handed. Offer them a drink and a snack. And, in general, be sure to only sing carols at Christmastime.

While it may be a time-honored tradition among older generations, 53 percent of 16-to-24-year-old English citizens admit that they dislike Christmas pudding.

A Revolutionary Christmas

General George Washington wasn't dreaming of a white Christmas when he decided to spring a surprise holiday attack on the British in 1776. Lucky for him, he got one—and a victory, too.

In December 1776 General Washington and his troops needed a miracle. Since the Battle of Long Island in August 1776, the British army had the Continental army on the run. They'd fled from New York through New Jersey and finally crossed the Delaware River to Pennsylvania (taking every boat available). The British were temporarily stuck on the Jersey side of the river, but once they overcame this temporary setback, they might deliver the final blow to the colonists.

The outcome of the War for Independence looked bleak. Through casualties, sickness, and desertion, Washington had lost 90 percent of his fighting force. American morale was low and sinking fast. Few soldiers were reenlisting, and most would go home at the end of the year when their tours of duty were up. A despairing Washington wrote to his brother, "I think the game is pretty near up."

A Glimmer of Hope

Despite grim prospects, there was hope. A spy brought
Washington news that the British forces planned to take a
few months off during the winter. The cold weather convinced the British commander, General Howe, that the strug-
gling American forces would be further weakened by the
frigid temperatures and would be easier to finish off in the
spring. Harsh weather or not, Washington recognized this
moment as an opportunity to turn things around. He could
move his troops against the British forces and their Hessian
mercenaries when the enemy would least suspect it:
Christmas seemed the perfect time.

Party on, Dudes

Colonel Johann Rall and his three garrisons stationed in
Trenton, New Jersey, had no worries about their enemies.
The Hessian forces planned on enjoying a merry Christmas
with feasts, parties, and drinking late into the night. On
Christmas, the colonel planned to celebrate at the home of a
friend. And he'd soundly dismissed the rebels: "Those clod-
hoppers will not attack us! And should they do so, we will
simply fall on them and rout them!"

Rall knew the outnumbered colonists were no match for the
disciplined Hessians in a straight fight. But Washington hoped
odds might be improved in an unexpected attack after the
enemy had celebrated Christmas with late-night parties and

plenty of beer. With any luck their enemy would be sleepy (and hungover) in the early morning hours of December 26.

A (Very) White Christmas

On December 25, Washington and his army wanted to cross the Delaware at sunset and surprise Rall's forces before dawn. But a terrible blizzard thwarted their plans. Ice and sleet made the crossing so difficult and time-consuming that it put the army hours behind schedule. Only one boat succeeded in crossing the river by 4 a.m.; the storm ultimately kept the other boats in Pennsylvania. Those who made it across then began a grueling nine-mile march to Trenton. Worst of all, although the colonists didn't know it, their boats had been spotted around midnight. Word of Washington's approach had been sent to Colonel Rall.

Christmas Cards

Colonel Rall was partying at his friend's home and deep in a card game when a Tory farmer showed up at the door. The overconfident Hessian commander was too absorbed in drinking and playing cards to speak to him, so the farmer left the servant a note with word of Washington's army heading to Trenton. Rall stuck the note in his waistcoat pocket without reading it and continued his Christmas cele- bration before retiring to bed.

The Continental army marched through the night. The

severe storm continued to rage and killed two men. But because of that very storm, the Hessians had canceled their usual predawn patrol, leaving the city unguarded. When the Continental army arrived undetected at 8:30 a.m., they were able to bring their cannons and artillery right into the streets of Trenton. The attack would be a surprise after all.

As the first shots were fired and the disorganized Hessians raced for their weapons, their commander was still sleeping off the previous night's endeavors. Alerted, Rall roused himself and groggily set out on horseback but was shot before he could rally his troops. The Americans moved quickly, as they surrounded the city. Within 90 minutes the battle was over. The Americans had won a battle that would reenergize the fight for independence.

As a triumphant Washington later wrote of his men, they "surrounded the Enemy and obliged 30 Officers and 886 privates to lay down their Arms without firing a Shot . . . took about, 900 prisoners." The only fatalities on the American side were the two deaths from cold and exposure. The Hessians suffered over 100 casualties.

One of the mortally wounded was Colonel Rall. An attending physician gave him the note from his pocket, and the Colonel realized what might have been. "If only I'd read this, I wouldn't be here," the commander lamented before he died.

The History of Santa, Part 2

*Two American artists inadvertently created the look of
Santa Claus—using a popular old poem, a bright color pallet,
and some ingenuity. (Part 1 appears on page 4.)*

In 1863, *Harper's Weekly* hired 21-year-old Thomas Nast to
draw a picture of Santa Claus bringing gifts to Union
troops fighting in the Civil War. The Santa that Nast drew
combined Clement Moore's description of Saint Nicholas from
his 1822 poem, "A Visit From Saint Nicholas" with, believe it
or not . . . Uncle Sam. Nast's Santa was a roly-poly old man
who wore a star-spangled jacket, striped pants, and a cap.

A New Look for an Old Man

The look was so popular that every year for 40 years, when
the magazine asked Nast to draw a Santa picture, he stuck to
the same concept—although he did drop the stars and stripes
in favor of a plain wool suit. Nast added new little details
every Christmas season: One year he showed Santa poring
over a list of naughty and nice children; another year Nast
showed him in a toy workshop at the North Pole. The
American public became accustomed to the image, and it was

gradually adopted into Americana. In fact, Nast is credited with single-handedly establishing the look of Santa as we know him. Except in one major area: the color of his suit. That was a product of Coca-Cola.

The Magic of Red

In 1931, Coca-Cola hired artist Haddon Sundblom to create the artwork for a massive Christmas advertising campaign they were preparing. Until then, the soda was primarily a summer drink, with sales dropping off sharply in the winter months. The company hoped to reverse this trend by linking the drink to the winter holidays, and they decided the most effective way to do that would be to make Santa Claus a Coke drinker.

Starting with the already familiar and beloved image of Nast's Santa, Sundblom decided to dump Nast's black-and-white Santa suit in favor of one in Coca-Cola red and white. It isn't difficult to imagine the rest. The new Santa emerged as a pink-cheeked, white-bearded old man with a twinkle in his eye, wearing a bright red suit, a big black belt, and tall black boots. He's been a permanent part of the American Christmas tradition ever since.

Criminal Christmas Capers

The weather outside is frightful, but the fire's so delightful, and since we've no place to go . . . let's rob a bank on Christmas! Okay, so it doesn't rhyme, but if watching a good holiday go bad appeals to you, here are films full of festive malfeasance.

Lethal Weapon (1987)

Christmastime is when two Los Angeles cops—Danny Glover and Mel Gibson—tangle with drug-smuggling ex–Special Forces officers. Mel Gibson's amusingly unhinged performance as a suicidal cop made him a superstar. But don't overlook Glover, whose stable family-man role allows Gibson the ability to go more than a little nuts. Still a classic in the action genre, and you won't have any trouble getting someone to watch it with you, even at Christmas.

Die Hard (1988)

It's an office Christmas party gone horribly wrong when ter-rorists, led by Alan Rickman, take over a high-rise and hold the partygoers hostage. Bruce Willis plays a cop who puts a big dent in their plans while delivering a lot of snarky one-liners. Big, loud, silly, violent, and a whole lot of fun. The

1990 sequel also takes place at Christmastime, which could be a sign that spending the holidays with Bruce Willis's character might be a dangerous idea.

Trapped in Paradise (1994)

This little film is about three criminal brothers attempting a heist in the small town of Paradise, Pennsylvania, where they get stuck and try to escape. The three crooks (played by Nicolas Cage, John Lovitz, and Dana Carvey) start to have second thoughts about their crime because the town is full of really, really nice folks. And it's Christmastime. While not exactly a classic, at least the movie's heart is in the right place.

The Ref (1994)

'Twas the night before Christmas, and a thief (Denis Leary) is in the house. He takes a posh Connecticut couple (Judy Davis and Kevin Spacey) hostage in order to hide out awhile; what he doesn't realize is that these people have more interpersonal issues than a dog has fleas—and the entire family's coming over for Christmas dinner! This underrated gem is sharp and witty, thanks to a great script (by Richard LaGravenese) and a trio of fine performances by Leary, Davis, and Spacey.

The Christmas Pickle

We've seen lots of Christmas ornaments: jolly Santas, ringing bells, sparkly snowflakes—but glass pickles? Why is that pickle on the Christmas tree?

What It Is: A blown-glass ornament of a green pickle.

Where It Came From: In Lauscha, Germany, local craftsmen first started making blown-glass ornaments in the shape of fruits and nuts in the mid-19th century. These ornaments were first imported into the United States in the 1880s and became very popular.

Why It Looks that Way: To give these glass ornaments their distinctive metallic appearance, they used a combination of pigment and mercury, lead, or silver nitrate to make the inside of the ornament shiny and colored.

How It Got on the Tree: According to ritual, on Christmas Eve the glass pickle should be the last ornament placed on the tree and should be hidden in its branches. The child who spots it first on Christmas morning will have a year of good luck, an extra present, or be allowed to open his gifts first.

Tannenbaumen Gone Red, White, and Blue

From the White House to the great sequoias in California, we've got some big and famous Christmas trees in the United States.

It's a Grand Ol' Tree

Though it may be low on the Christmas radar for most of us, the massive General Grant Tree, located in Kings Canyon National Park in California, has been America's official Christmas tree for some 80 years.

When Charles Lee of Sanger, California, visited the mammoth tree in the mid-1920s, he overheard a little girl say, "What a wonderful Christmas tree it would be." Liking the idea, Lee wrote to the president of the United States about it. Calvin Coolidge designated it the nation's Christmas tree in 1926; since then, a small group of hardy hikers have made their way to the tree each year for an annual Trek to the Tree celebration. The celebration includes Christmas music and speeches, and every year a large wreath is placed at the base of the tree.

A couple fun facts: The General Grant Tree is the third-largest tree in the world. It stands 267 feet tall, is 40 feet across its base, and is more than 107 feet around. Scientists estimate the giant sequoia to be between 1,500 and 2,000 years old.

The General Grant Tree serves a dual purpose as both the National Christmas Tree and the only living national shrine dedicated to the memory of soldiers who have died in any U.S. war (a distinction it received in 1956).

Christmas at the White House

Every year since 1961, in a tradition begun by Jacqueline Kennedy, the First Lady has chosen a theme for the official White House tree. A "Nutcracker Suite" tree was Jacqueline Kennedy's classy choice to launch the new tradition. Since then, there have been a wide variety of themes—some glitzy, some ritzy. In 2001, Laura Bush's decorations consisted of tiny replicas of presidential family homes in "Home for the Holidays." Knitted mittens and caps adorned the 1998 "Winter Wonderland" tree by Hillary Rodham Clinton, and the needlepoint figurines in the 1991 "Noah's Ark"–themed tree were special favorites of Barbara Bush.

Some years, White House trees have had ornaments made and donated by special-interest groups around the county. The disabled men and women of the National Association of Retarded Citizens made the trimmings for President Carter's White House tree in 1977. And a group of disabled workers from Florida made balls that represented each of the 50 states and presented them to President Nixon for the 1969 tree.

The tree isn't the only thing decorated in the White House. For Christmas 2003, White House decor consisted of 70,000 lights, 19 trees, 660 feet of garland, 245 wreaths, 251 bows, and two antique sleighs. Some 45 volunteers helped to get the mansion ready for its estimated 37,000 holiday visitors.

The Tree in the Big Apple

It may be hard to imagine, but back in 1930 there wasn't a Rockefeller Center Christmas Tree. There wasn't even a Rockefeller Center. During the 1931 holiday season, though, things changed. That year, construction workers laboring over the site of the new Rockefeller Center put up a small tree, hastily decorated it, and then got in line for their paychecks—there was a depression going on, after all. A tradition was born—weak as it was—and New Yorkers have never looked back.

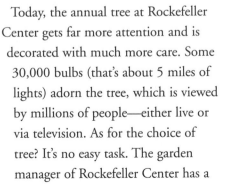

Today, the annual tree at Rockefeller Center gets far more attention and is decorated with much more care. Some 30,000 bulbs (that's about 5 miles of lights) adorn the tree, which is viewed by millions of people—either live or via television. As for the choice of tree? It's no easy task. The garden manager of Rockefeller Center has a yearlong project at hand. With the use of a helicopter, he scours the countryside searching for the perfect tree to grace the honored holiday spot in New York City. Qualifications for the tree include it being tall and full with no drooping in the branches, and having a healthy, dark green coloring. Once a tree is selected, the garden manager approaches the owner (trees are often selected from people's yards) and asks permission to cut down the tree—without compensation. It's fairly routine. Few people would decline such an honor. Once the decision has been made, a police officer is deployed to guard the tree, in case someone decides to put up a fuss and climb the tree before the tree cutters come to haul it away.

The tree is recycled after the holiday season. In years past, it has been donated to the Boy Scouts, to the U.S. Equestrian Team for horse jumps, the Appalachian Trail for chips, even to the zoo to be turned into animal shapes for kids.

The Christmas Comet

Edmond Halley had a theory about comet sitings in 1456, 1531, 1607, and 1682. Scientists of the time thought that these were separate comets, but Halley knew the sitings were all of the same comet. He predicted that the comet would return in 1758. His prediction came true, and Halley's comet was spotted on Christmas Day, 1758. But Halley didn't live to see its return; he died in 1742.

Christmas in History

Big things happen on this Christian holiday.

On December 25, A.D. 800, Charlemagne was crowned emperor of the Holy Roman Empire by Pope Leo III.

On Christmas Day in 1066, William the Conqueror was crowned king of England.

On Christmas Eve in 1814, the United States and Britain signed the Treaty of Ghent to end the War of 1812.

On Christmas Eve 1968, *Apollo 8* became the first manned mission to reach and orbit the Moon. Frank Borman, James A. Lovell Jr., and William Anders went around it 10 times that December 24th.

On Christmas Day 1938, David O. Selznick asked Vivian Leigh to play Scarlett O'Hara in *Gone With the Wind.* Guess he didn't want to think about it tomorrow.

Putting a Stamp on Christmas

Did you know that Canada issued the world's first Christmas stamp in December 1898? It may sound festive, but it was more of a happy accident than a celebration of the holiday season.

In 1898, British lawmakers decided to implement a uniform postage rate for the colonies; the new rate would let anyone in the colonies send a letter anywhere in the British Empire for just a penny. Each colony could design its own stamp, but it still needed to secure Queen Victoria's approval.

The Map Stamp

William Mulock, Canada's postmaster general, helped design a Canadian stamp that reflected the grandeur of the British Empire and promoted the new uniform rate. Referred to now as the Map Stamp, Canada's stamp depicted a world map with all of the British colonies colored red. The tagline, "We Hold A Vaster Empire Than Has Ever Been," was taken from "A Song of Empire," composed in honor of the 50th anniversary of Queen Victoria's reign. Since the stamp glorified the British Empire and its monarch, it seemed certain to secure the royal seal of approval.

So how did Christmas get involved with this decidedly non-Christmasy postage stamp? When the Duke of Norfolk, Great Britain's postmaster general, presented the Canadian stamp to Queen Victoria, she asked him when the stamp would be issued. Since the new postage rate was to come into effect on November 9, 1898, the birthday of Edward, the Prince of Wales, he answered, "On the prince's birthday." A bit miffed since she had four sons and he had not specified which one, the queen replied, "Which prince?" The duke, recovering quickly from his presumptive error, answered, "The Prince of Peace," which placated the queen. "XMAS 1898" was added, and the first Christmas stamp was born.

Postscript

- Canada didn't issue a Christmas stamp again until 1964. This time the stamp was clearly designed for the holidays: It depicted a family admiring the star of Bethlehem.

- In 2004, Canada Post produced four designs for their Christmas stamps and printed over 65 million stamps.

- Before the United States issued its first Christmas stamps in 1962, places such as Austria (1937), Brazil (1939), Hungary (1941), Cuba (1951), and Haiti (1954) already had their own.

- Today more than 200 countries issue Christmas stamps.

Gifts of Christmas Past: The 1990s

From the decade that brought us Crystal Pepsi and the Spice Girls, here are some hot holiday gifts of the 1990s.

1990

A new group of collectable dolls showed the right stuff this year: the New Kids on the Block. Yes, the posable doll versions of the late-80s boy band were among the hottest toys of the year.

1991

The long national nightmare that was known as "hair metal" came to a screeching halt when the two albums that defined grunge rock found their way under the tree: Nirvana's *Nevermind,* with its instant classic hit "Smells Like Teen Spirit" and Pearl Jam's *Ten,* with its hits "Alive" and "Jeremy."

1992

This was the year of monster authors. Danielle Steele, Stephen King, and John Grisham slugged it our for bestseller supremacy. (Steele with *Mixed Blessing* and *Jewels,* King with

Dolores Claiborne and *Gerald's Game*, and Grisham with *The Pelican Brief*.) In non-fiction, gruff conservatives and military buffs got a holiday double shot from Rush Limbaugh's *The Way Things Ought to Be* and General Norman Schwarzkopf's *It Doesn't Take a Hero*.

1993
Nothing says toy sales like teenagers in multicolored unitards, which may be why the Mighty Morphin Power Rangers toys were such a huge hit.

1994
New fragrances DK Men (Donna Karan), Tommy (Tommy Hilfiger) and Blue Jeans (Versace) duked it out with traditional favorites Old Spice and Polo for the gift for dads everywhere.

1995
This holiday season saw the peak of Pogs. The game of disc flipping got its start back in the 1930s, but it wasn't until the 1990s that the game became an international craze—and then became passe just as quickly.

1996
The vocal and vibrating Tickle Me Elmo was so popular it was almost impossible to buy, leading desperate parents to pay hundreds of dollars for a stuffed toy with a $29.99 price tag.

USA Today noted that national retailer Target sold 50,000 of the toys in just four hours. A toy store in Camden, New Jersey, sold 100 of the toys in just four minutes.

1997

Some 40 million Tamagotchis—little virtual pets—made their way into stockings nationwide. Millions of children who couldn't be relied on to feed a hamster or fish obsessively tended to these electronic animals with a life span of just a few weeks.

1998

Furbys—creepy little animals that learn to speak English and communicate with other Furbys by way of infrared ports in their foreheads, swept the nation. They were even banned from U.S. intelligence agency offices because of the mistaken belief that the little creatures could repeat words spoken to them.

1999

Pokémon invaded the nation with their cuteness and the exhortation by their owner Nintendo that kids and fans "Gotta Catch Them All!" And since there are nearly 400 of the little creatures, across various toy, card game, and video game lines, that's a lot of sales—over 100 million Pokémon games and toys sold worldwide.

Festive Feasting on Christmas Eve

Christmas Day may be the main event, but there's some good eating to be done on Christmas Eve around the world.

Les Treize Desserts

If you like dessert, the Provence region of France is the place to be on Christmas Eve. There, revelers serve 13 desserts after midnight mass. Each dish in Les Treize Desserts symbolizes either Jesus or one of his 12 disciples. Types of desserts do vary from house to house, but there are four common ones. Collectively called the mendicants, figs, raisins, hazelnuts, and almonds each stand for the color of the robes of a certain monastic order: Franciscans (figs), Dominicans (raisins), Augustines (hazelnuts), and Carmelites (almonds). Another tradition of the meal is to break all breads by hand (no cutting allowed) to insure a bountiful harvest in the new year.

A Dip, Dip Here . . . A Dip, Dip There

In Sweden, the Christmas Eve tradition is a communal one called Doppa i Grytan, which translates to "dipping in the kettle." Family and friends gather to dip pieces of rye bread into a pot of juices and drippings from roasted meats and sausages. The tradition is so popular that Christmas Eve is sometimes called Dipping Day.

One Fish, Two Fish . . .

On Christmas Eve, many Italians sit down to La Vigilia, or the Feast of the Fishes, a tradition believed to come from Sicily. The broad concept is simple enough: Each course of the meal highlights a different type of fish. But the exact number and meaning of the dishes is difficult to pin down. Some serve 7 fishes, some 10, and others 13 fishes. The number 7 can symbolize the 7 deadly sins, the 7 sacraments of the Catholic Church, the 7 days that Mary and Joseph traveled to Bethlehem, or even the 7 hills of Rome. Ten stands for the stations of the cross. And 13 would be the number of disciples plus Jesus. Whatever the number, that's a lot of fish!

"Mail your packages early so the post office can lose them in time for Christmas."

—*Johnny Carson, comedian*

The Real North Poles

Everyone knows Santa lives at the North Pole, but how do they know which one?

North Pole 1

This is a fixed point on the earth's surface—and the imaginary line that runs from it, straight through the earth to the South Pole, forms the axis of the earth. Many people think the ice that covers the North Pole has land beneath it, but it doesn't. This North Pole sits atop a floating 6–10 foot thick ice cap over the Arctic Ocean, so there's nothing but frigid water underneath.

North Pole 2

The second pole is magnetic. It's the North Pole that compasses point toward, but its physical location can move anywhere from 6 to 25 miles a day. (The earth's polarity is affected by molten metal underground and charged particles from the sun.) Currently, North Pole 2 is about 600 miles from North Pole 1.

North Pole 3, 4, 5, & 6

In the United States, there are also four towns that go by the name North Pole. There's one in New York, Idaho, Oklahoma, and Alaska. Alaska's is just 1,700 miles from the terrestrial North Pole and is dedicated to all things Christmas. Founded in

1944, North Pole, Alaska, was originally supposed to be a toy-manufacturing center, but the venture never took off. Instead, it evolved into a theme town where "the spirit of Christmas lives year round." Streets have Yuletide names like Snowman Lane and Saint Nicholas Drive. This North Pole is also home to the Santa Claus House and a post office that receives as many as 100,000 "Dear Santa" letters every year.

"Christmas is a time when kids tell Santa what they want and adults pay for it. Deficits are when adults tell the government what they want—and their kids pay for it."

—*Richard Lamm,*
former governor of Colorado

Bright Ideas

Christmas lights are among the first things towns bring out to welcome the holiday season. And most of us have grown up with the tradition of stringing lights around our houses and yards. But all that began long after we started stringing lights on trees.

Hold a Candle to It

According to popular legend, the first Christmas tree was illuminated in the mid-1500s when Martin Luther placed candles on a tree to capture the look of the night sky in Bethlehem. But that's only a myth; no one knows now if it really happened. It wasn't until a couple hundred years later that there is documented evidence that candles were used to light up ole Tannenbaum. In those days the candles were attached to branches with wax or pins, but they were a big fire hazard. Glass balls and minilanterns were used as candleholders in the early 1900s to prevent the open flames from setting fire to the trees, but they weren't always effective. And they were a big nuisance—someone always had to be on guard to keep the flames from spreading.

Tripping the Light Fantastic

Thomas Edison's invention of a lasting lightbulb arguably began the trend for Christmas lights. In 1882 Edward Johnson, one of Edison's assistants, used a wire to wrap colored lightbulbs around the Christmas tree in his home. By the end of the 1800s, General Electric had bought the rights to mass-produce the wired Christmas bulbs, and in 1895 President Grover Cleveland had the White House tree outfitted with lights. The American public took interest in this bright new phenomenon. But the early strings of lights were costly—about $300, roughly $2,000 by today's standards—so only the rich could afford them.

E Pluribus Christmas

It wasn't until 1917 that Albert Sadacca, a young Spanish immigrant living in New York, found a way to bring the lights to the masses. His family's business consisted of selling novelty wicker birdcages lit by lightbulbs, and he suggested putting the spare bulbs on strings to wind them around Christmas trees. Now, people could purchase them for a reasonable price, and it didn't take long for the lights to become a huge success. The lights ultimately generated millions of dollars in sales for Sadacca's new venture, NOMA Corporation. It was the first to introduce "bubble lights" to the world, in 1946. Until 1965, NOMA was the leading Christmas lights manufacturer. Several companies in Taiwan and China now compete for the spot that NOMA held for so many years.

Santa Surveillance

Children don't have to search the darkened skies on Christmas Eve for a glimpse of Santa's sleigh. NORAD's got a high-tech solution to keeping tabs on Santa Claus.

Sorry, Wrong Number

It all began in 1955 with a wrong number. In Colorado Springs, Colorado, a local department store ran a Christmas advertisement that featured a Santa Claus hotline. The problem? The printed number connected callers to the Continental Air Defense Command (CADC), not Santa Claus. The senior officer on duty that Christmas Eve, Colonel Harry Shoup, was a little flummoxed when he started receiving calls from kids asking for Santa. After quickly figuring out the situation, Shoup told the children that he was working for Santa and tracking his sleigh on the radar. In the days following, the local news media broke the story of the phone calls, and a holiday tradition was born.

Yes, Virginia, There Is a Santa Claus Tracker

The North American Aerospace Defense Command (NORAD), successor to the CADC, took over the tracking duties in 1957 and has been monitoring Santa's annual ride ever since. The U.S.–Canadian military organization monitors the air and space defenses of North America year-round from its location in Cheyenne Mountain in Colorado. But on December 24, attention turns to the fat man in the red suit. Why? Master Sergeant John Tomassi, deputy head of Santa Tracking Operations in 2004, says it's because "we want to make sure he gets around the world all right." So how does NORAD do it? Its key methods are the following:

- **Radar:** NORAD's "North Warning" radar system comprises 47 installations that begin monitoring Santa as soon as he leaves the North Pole on December 24.

- **Satellites:** Able to detect missiles by the heat their launches create, satellites track the infrared heat emitted by Santa's famous, red-nosed reindeer. One veteran tracker claims that the more carrots Rudolph eats, the brighter his nose glows.

- **Jet Fighters:** These escorts are F/A-18 Hornets (also called CF-18s), while in Canadian airspace, and either F-15 Eagles or F-16 Fighting Falcons, over the United States. Though NORAD estimates that Santa travels about 600 times the speed of light—300 times faster than these planes—he does slow down to wave to the pilots.

- **Santa Cams:** Both mounted on NORAD fighter jets and positioned in various grounded locations around the

globe, these digital cameras are able catch video and still images of Kris Kringle.

Keeping Up With the Claus

Those interested in checking on Santa's Christmas Eve progress have two options available to them: the phone (toll-free at 1-877-HI-NORAD) and the Internet (www.noradsanta.com). Launched in 1997, the Web site was an immediate success. During its first Christmas Eve, 10 million viewers tried to access the site (only 1 million got through). Since then, the online system has been substantially improved to handle all the traffic, which has grown over the years. In 2004, NORAD successfully fielded 50,000 e-mails and 600 million hits. Visitors can also see up-to-the-minute radar maps and streaming video from the current ride. Tracking Santa has become a global phenomenon; now Santa updates are available in six languages: English, French, Italian, Japanese, Spanish, and Portuguese. So no matter the language, everyone can make sure they're in bed before Santa gets to their time zone.

Pop! Goes the Cracker

When pulled apart, the Christmas cracker pops open to reveal a variety of surprises inside. It seems simple enough, but it took a lot of time and effort to get the cracker into its present form.

The idea first began to take shape in the 1840s, thanks to the creative genius of an English confectioner named Thomas Smith. Unlike many of his contemporaries who churned out the same cakes and pastries every day, Smith was always on the lookout for something new.

The French Connection

On a trip to Paris in 1840, Smith tasted a bonbon, a sugared almond wrapped in a twist of colorful tissue paper. Smith brought some of the treats home and put them in a display in his shop; he was thrilled by how well they sold that Christmas season. And Smith was paying very close attention. He noted that most of the candies were bought by men for their sweethearts, so he began including love quotes in the brightly colored wrappers. Sales continued to rise.

Smith knew he was onto something big and he wanted to develop his idea even further, but he was unable to come up with anything suitable. Then one evening he observed the crackle of a log in his fireplace. That was it! He would make the wrappers pop when they were opened.

It's a Snap

Smith went to work experimenting with various cracking mechanisms, and expanded the size and nature of the packaging. Eventually he discovered that by pasting small strips of potassium nitrate to two strips of cardboard he could create a cracking noise when the strips were forcibly pulled apart. He named his new invention Cosaques, alluding to the crack of a Cossack's whip, and brought them to market. To his delight, the public loved them.

Over time, Smith continued to tinker with his creation, adding a surprise gift and decorative tissue hats to the contents of the cracker. By 1900, his growing business was selling more than 13 million crackers annually and was even creating special designs to commemorate world fairs and coronations. Tom Smith Group Ltd. is still the world's

largest manufacturer of Christmas crackers. The company now exports its product to more than 34 countries. If you're lucky, they've even graced the table of your own Christmas feast.

The Return of
the Yuletide Yuk

Our final installment of some corny holiday jokes.

Why does Santa have three gardens?
So he can ho-ho-ho.

What do you get if you cross a snowman and a shark?
Frostbite.

What did Adam say on the day before Christmas?
"It's Christmas, Eve."

Why was Santa's little helper depressed?
Because he had low elf-esteem.

What was so good about the neurotic doll the girl was given
for Christmas?
It was wound up already.

What do you call Santa's helpers?
Subordinate clauses.

Holiday Word Search

This Christmas stocking is filled with good stuff! Finding the 28 holiday words and phrases herein might be easier than locating that must-have gift.

BAH HUMBUG	NOEL
CARDS	NORTH POLE
CAROLS	ORNAMENTS
CHIMNEY	PEACE ON EARTH
EGGNOG	POINSETTIA
ELVES	SANTA CLAUS
GIFTS	SCROOGE
HOLLY	ST NICK
HOLY NIGHT	TINSEL
JACK FROST	TINY TIM
MANGER	TOYS
MERRY CHRISTMAS	TREE
MISTLETOE	XMAS
NATIVITY	YULE LOG

Turn to page 178 for the answers.

```
            P  E  A  C  E  O  N  E  A  R  T  H  M  C
            Q  O  S  F  T  R  A  L  M  E  I  O  R  X
            S  M  I  V  L  N  C  V  D  U  B  L  T  Y
            F  Z  C  N  O  A  L  E  R  T  F  Y  Z  P
            N  M  O  A  S  M  W  S  L  E  S  N  I  T
            Y  E  U  T  X  E  M  I  T  Y  N  I  T  E
            L  X  A  I  B  N  T  G  O  N  G  G  E  W
               F  V  L  T  R  T  Q  X  A  H
               I  I  W  S  V  X  I  B  S  T
               M  T  I  Y  S  W  Z  A  A  K
               J  Y  P  K  P  R  N  H  Z  T
               G  L  G  T  S  T  G  H  M  S
               O  S  D  R  A  C  V  U  A  O
               L  K  E  C  M  W  B  M  N  R
               E  Q  L  C  T  P  X  B  G  F
               L  A  O  K  S  M  R  U  E  K
               U  D  P  E  I  H  F  G  R  C
            S  Y  Y  H  S  R  Q  K  U  D  A
         B  M  L  L  T  A  H  X  Y  B  E  J
      D  S  R  F  L  R  N  C  A  R  O  L  S
   A  W  C  V  E  O  O  C  Y  W  K  T  U
   P  X  R  T  L  H  N  E  R  V  Z  L  P
R  V  M  O  L  K  R  N  X  R  K  F  C
Q  Y  E  O  A  M  M  T  R  E  E  T
S  B  X  G  G  I  F  T  S  M  H
T  F  C  E  H  U  W  L  B  W
   U  K  C  I  N  T  S  Z
   R  M  Z  K  O  Y
   V  B  A  B
```

Christmas Characters

18-Across might strain your memory, but you can probably get the answers from the crossers. The other four Christmas characters here include three Dickens creations, and one holiday reindeer.

ACROSS

1	Soak, as bread in gravy
4	Domain
9	Olin and Horne
14	Heavy wts.
15	Toulouse toodle-oo
16	"Für ___ " (Beethoven dedication)
17	Sailor's yes
18	Natalie Wood's character in *Miracle on 34th Street*
20	Not polished
22	Hinged item in some cabs
23	He'll go down in history
26	"Peg ___ Heart" (1947 Harmonicats hit)
27	Green people
29	Sake
34	Rock's Bon ___
37	R & B singer James
39	Big Gateway user
40	Meanie redeemed in *A Christmas Carol*
43	Somewhat, colloquially
44	Corleone's bodyguard, ___ Brasi
45	Take it easy
46	Pavarotti, Domingo, and Carreras

48	Toy-truck maker
50	Confession starter
52	He says, "God bless us every one!"
56	Symbols of welcome
61	"___ Mio"
62	Clerk for 40-Across and father of 52-Across
65	Cockpit stat
66	Rockabilly's Chris
67	Be there in spirit?
68	Fed. money lender
69	Old gas burners
70	Clear out
71	Phone abbr.

DOWN

1	Outlaw Belle
2	"The joke's ___!"
3	False front?
4	How some people get tattoos
5	School domain, on the Net
6	Sue Grafton's "___ for Alibi"
7	Go ahead
8	Author Alice
9	2000, for one
10	Building wings
11	Goddess of victory

Turn to page 178 for the answers.

12	On a yacht
13	Spanish muralist
19	Gestation location
21	Entered
24	Bush, slangily, with *The*
25	Marvin Gardens buy
28	Swagger
30	Cheers
31	Soothing botanical
32	Staying power
33	Guitar ridge
34	Rib-tickler
35	Slender reed
36	Country singer Gosdin
38	Classy tie
41	Tags
42	"What ___ say?"
47	Word in a Doris Day song
49	Hard to saw, as some pine
51	Beatles classic "I ___ Walrus"
53	Done for, in slang
54	"Well, ___—!" ("Holy cow!")
55	Gold or silver
56	Off-Broadway Tony
57	General Foods founder
58	Israel's Abba
59	College sports org.
60	Shell game
63	Cadence call
64	What savings accts. pay

Answer Pages

Annual Animated Offerings: A Triple-Threat Quiz, page 14

1. Burl Ives

   II. Sam

   C. *Rudolph the Red-Nosed Reindeer*

2. Fred Astaire

   III. S. D. Kluger

   A. *Santa Claus Is Comin' to Town*

3. Buddy Hackett

   IV. Pardon-Me-Pete

   B. *Jack Frost*

4. Roger Miller

   V. Speiltoe

   D. *Nestor the Long-Eared Christmas Donkey*

5. Red Skelton

   I. Father Time

   E. *Rudolph's Shiny New Year*

Cartoon Christmas: A Triple-Threat Quiz, page 104

1. Drew Barrymore

V. Olive

    C. *Olive, the Other Reindeer*

2. Jimmy Durante

    IV. The Narrator

    D. *Frosty the Snowman*

3. Boris Karloff

    II. The Grinch

    A. *How the Grinch Stole Christmas*

4. Joel Grey

    I. Joshua Trundle

    E. *'Twas the Night Before Christmas*

5. Jim Backus

    III. Ebenezer Scrooge

    B. *Mr. Magoo's Christmas Carol*

Test Your Christmas IQ, page 118

1. D. None

2. B. Oklahoma

3. D. German settlers

4. A. "Why are there other Santas at other malls?"

5. A. *Harper's Weekly*

6. C. Gene Autry

7. A. Constantine (The Great)

8. D. Roman

9. B. Finland

Holiday Word Search, page 172

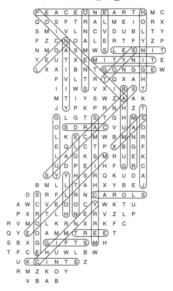

Christmas Characters, page 174

S	O	P		R	E	A	L	M		L	E	N	A	S
T	N	S		A	D	I	E	U		E	L	I	S	E
A	Y	E		S	U	S	A	N	W	A	L	K	E	R
R	O	U	G	H			D	R	O	P	S	E	A	T
R	U	D	O	L	P	H		O	M	Y				
'		T	Y	R	O	S		B	E	H	A	L	F	
J	O	V	I		E	T	T	A		A	O	L	E	R
E	B	E	N	E	Z	E	R	S	C	R	O	O	G	E
S	O	R	T	A		L	U	C	A		R	E	S	T
T	E	N	O	R	S		T	O	N	K	A			
			M	E	A		T	I	N	Y	T	I	M	
O	P	E	N	A	R	M	S			O	S	O	L	E
B	O	B	C	R	A	T	C	H	I	T		A	L	T
I	S	A	A	K		H	A	U	N	T		S	B	A
E	T	N	A	S		E	M	P	T	Y		T	E	L